Xiomara Maldonado Cruz, photographed in the doorway of her house in Utuado

This book is dedicated
with affection to everyone for whom
the island of Puerto Rico is
Borinquen Querida

Antique map of the Caribbean: the Library of Congress, Washington, D.C.

Fringed by some of the finest beaches of Puerto Rico and the Caribbean, the island of Vieques lies some 10 miles east of the main island. Like its smaller sister, Culebra, 10 miles to the north, Vieques is part of Puerto Rico although geologically more similar to the Virgin Islands group just a few miles to the east.

Puerto Rico, Borinquen Querida

Text and photographs by
Roger A. LaBrucherie

Imágenes Press

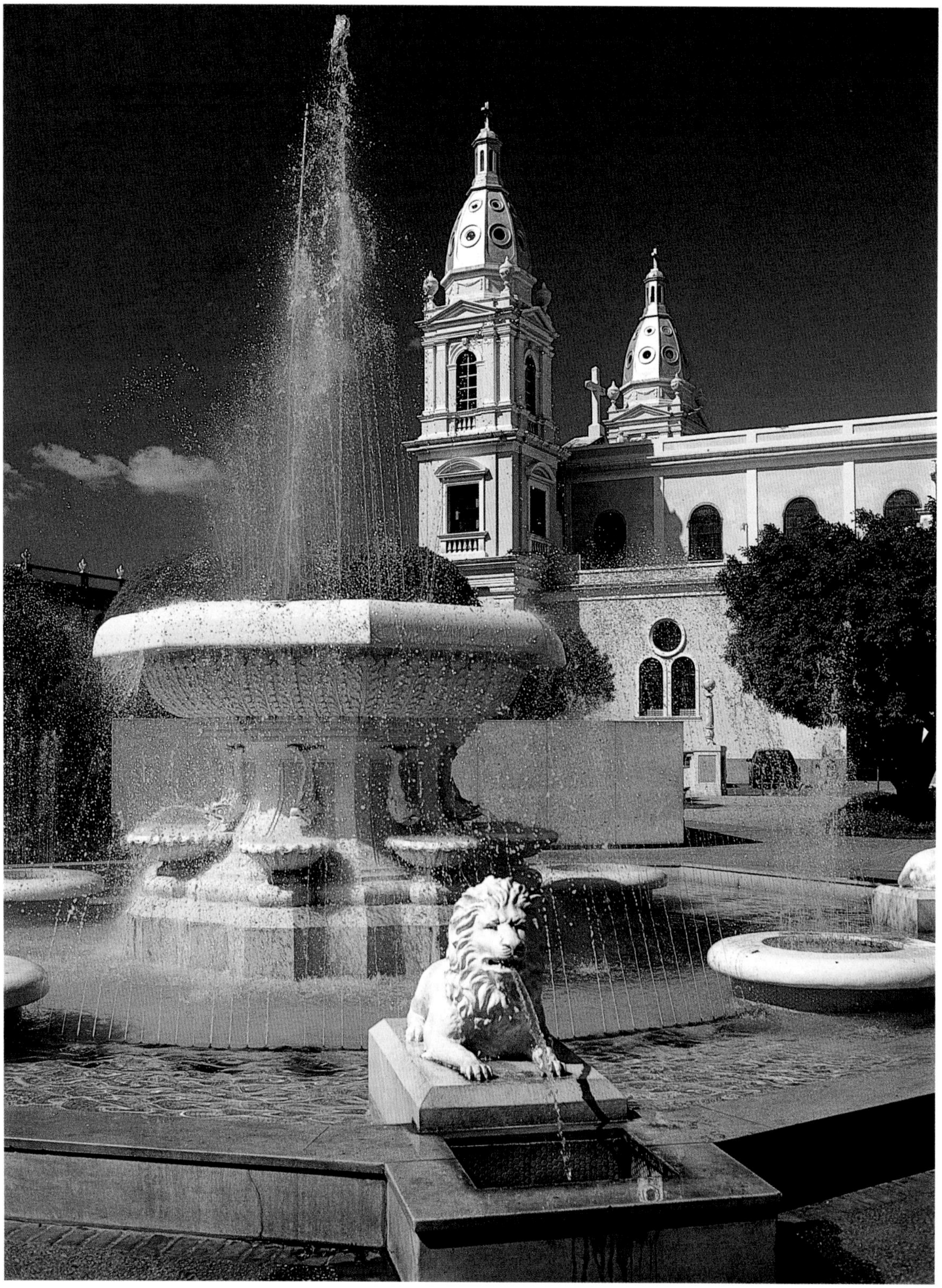

A fountain dances before the Nuestra Señora de Guadalupe Cathedral in Ponce's Parque de las Delicias.

Foreword

Astonishing though it sometimes is to me, nearly a decade has passed since I began the research and photography for my first book on the island, *Images of Puerto Rico.* Despite, or perhaps because of, the splendid reception accorded that book, I have long wanted to produce a book emphasizing my favorite visual aspects of the island: her natural scenic beauty and the finest examples of architecture from the Spanish colonial period.

In spite of a narrower focus, this volume shares a common philosophical underpinning with its predecessor: that is, to communicate a deeper understanding of a place, its people and culture to the tourist or new-arrival which will enable him to see beyond the "post-card" image which he is likely to bring with him.

Nowhere, and at no time, I think, is that attempt at cross-cultural education more vital than with Puerto Rico today, caught as it is between two diverse cultures, and constantly subject to the scrutiny and judgment of visitors with often only a scant understanding of the island and its people. In a world growing ever smaller, outsiders, and especially mainland Americans, will increasingly be called upon to understand Puerto Rico and her unique culture.

The confusion and lack of comprehension on the part of outsiders is understandable in view of the essential dichotomy of Puerto Rico's relationship with the United States. Within American jurisdiction, as reflected in a common citizenship, flag, currency, and numerous applicable Federal laws, Puerto Rico often seems in everything but name a State of the Union. And on the other side of the dichotomy, a culture and society profoundly different from that of the mainland.

Apart from the very obvious difference of the dominant language, many of these cultural differences are harder to specify and quantify than are the formal elements in common just mentioned, perhaps especially because of a modern tendency to stress that all mankind is the same. While at a fundamental human level this may be true, it is surely counterproductive to deny that at a social and cultural level profound differences exist between peoples of very different backgrounds.

It may seem presumptuous that a primarily pictorial book should open by raising questions which a reader might more naturally expect to find in a scholarly work on the sociology or culture of Puerto Rico. I do not for a moment pretend that this book is such a work; and yet I feel compelled to suggest that *Puerto Rico, Borinquen Querida* is at least somewhat informed by a strong awareness of the cultural complexity of the Puerto Rican scene.

My experience with the island began just over twenty years ago, when I spent several memorable months in Ponce in training for my service as a Peace Corps Volunteer. Over the ensuing two decades since that initial encounter I have spent many more months in Puerto Rico, photographing, interviewing, and researching the material for my two books about the island, and additional months off-island researching original and secondary sources. Thus, while I do not claim academic credentials in Puerto Rican history or culture, neither is it fair to say that my contact with the island has been fleeting.

One result of this extended relationship with Puerto Rico has been the growing realization that, the better I come to know her, the more complex I realize her culture and society to be. And from it, too, I realize that if outsiders are ever to hope to understand Puerto Rico and her culture, they must above all come to an understanding of the Puerto Ricans' deep pride in their island and their heritage. It is my hope that both the words and the photographs of this book will contribute to an understanding of that pride.

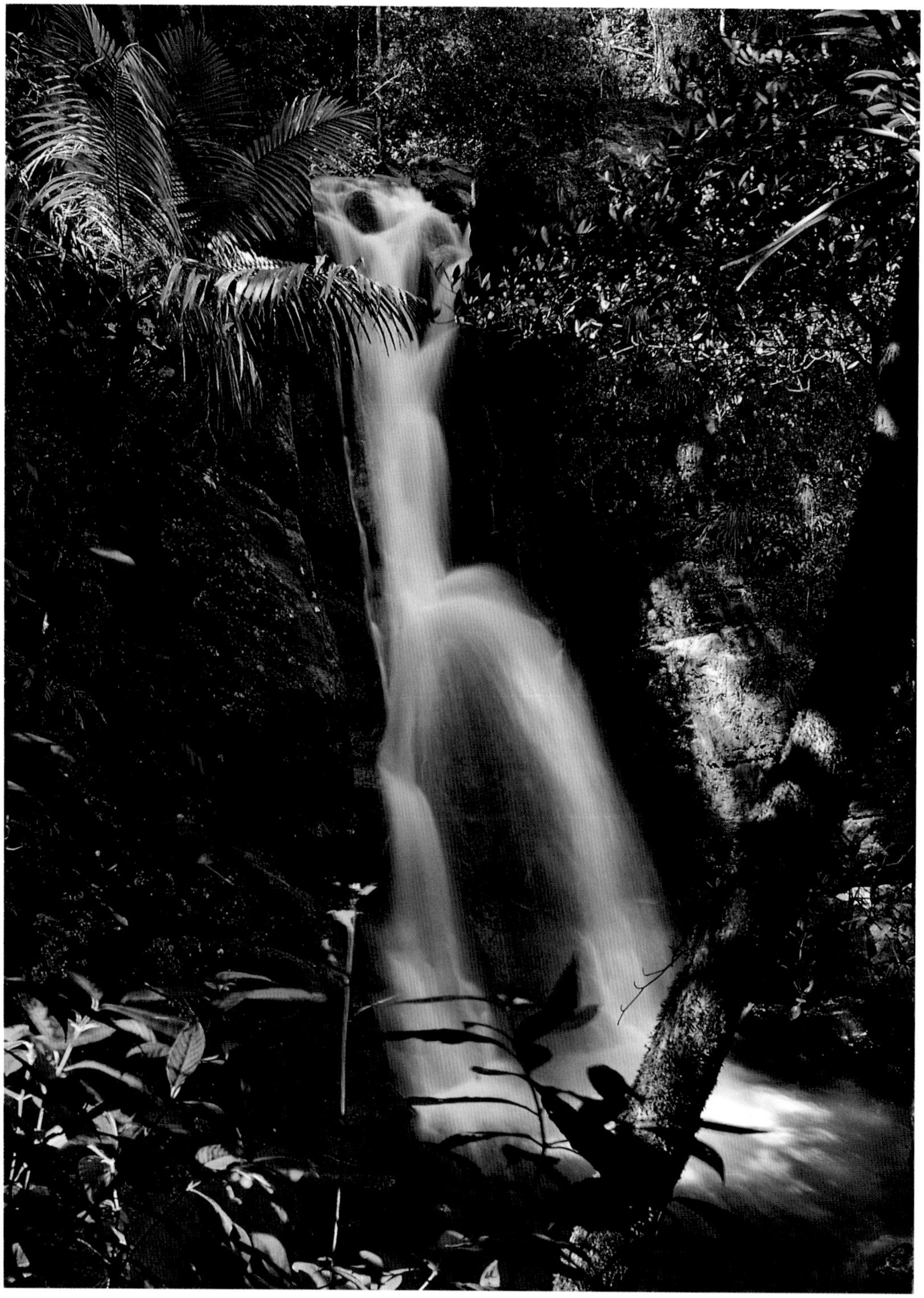

La Mina Falls cascades into the quiet of the El Yunque Rain Forest high in the Sierra de Luquillo.

Contents

Worlds Collide

Emerald isles, fringed by unblemished white-sand shores, floating in a crystalline blue sea—for time beyond comprehension this eden had evolved. Then massive forces deep within the earth pushed enormous mountains up from the sea floor. Tropical rains over seamless time eroded these mountains into a precipitous landscape. Wind and current and an occasional bird brought the first seeds, spreading plant life along the two thousand miles of island arc joining the continents lying to the northwest and south, until the islands were carpets of vegetation. As this lush paradise took form, the first birds and insects, carried perhaps by fierce winds, reached the islands and made them their home. At great intervals lizards, iguanas and frogs managed to survive a sea journey aboard a piece of driftwood, find a mate, and establish themselves on the island. For eons this eden was shaped, oblivious to the lands beyond its encompassing azure sea.

Oceans away, perhaps 400,000 years ago, the earliest humans were evolving and spreading across Africa, Asia, and Europe. Only much later, perhaps ten thousand years before the birth of Christ, did the first tribes venture across the land bridge which intermittently linked Asia with Alaska, and slowly begin spreading throughout the twin continents of the Western Hemisphere.

Then, when North and South America had been peopled for millennia, a people referred to by anthropologists as belonging to the Archaic culture began exploring the links of that island chain joining the two continents. Whether they worked their way south and east from Florida or north and west from South America has not been established with certainty (the present weight of opinion leans toward Florida), but it is fairly well established that they had reached Puerto Rico in the few centuries before the time of Christ.

The Archaic economy was heavily based on fishing, and some hunting and gathering, and the evidence of their presence on the island, scant though it is, has been found primarily in or near a coastal cave known as María La Cruz near Loíza, east of San Juan. The duration of the Archaic presence in Puerto Rico is unknown, although the fact that they were a non-agricultural, semi-nomadic people suggests that they would not have built settlements of great permanence in any case.

The second culture to occupy the island was the Igneri, or Saladoid, another fishing-hunting society, but one which certainly reached the island from the south, originating in the Saladoid region of the Orinoco Valley of Venezuela and spreading its way up the island chain of the Lesser Antilles. Even though the Igneris endured on the island

In a scene little changed since the Taino Indians ruled the island, another dawn comes to the north coast near Punta Manatí.

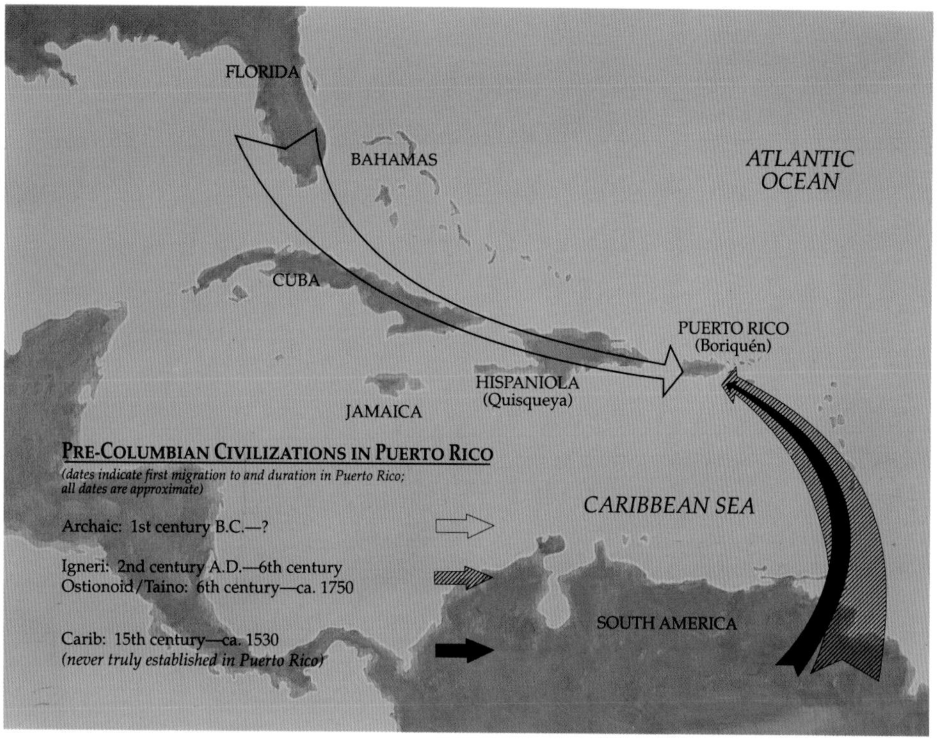

Puerto Rico was host to a succession of Indian cultures: the first was the Archaic, which originated in Florida and reached the island before the time of Christ. Six hundred years later the first of the Taino emigrations arrived from South America, and it was the Taino ancestral name for the island, Boriquén, *which would survive (slightly modified) into the present day and become the affectionate name for Puerto Rico.*

The most spectacular remains of Taino culture are the bateyes, *or ceremonial ball courts, such as those uncovered and restored near Utuado [opposite page].*

some four hundred years, or until about the Sixth Century A.D., little is known of their culture, save the fact that they excelled in pottery-making, based on their artifacts.

About the time the Igneri culture entered into decline another culture, the Ostionoid, spread northward along the same route from the Orinoco Valley. Like the Igneris, the Ostionoids were a subgroup of the Arawak Indian culture which occupied much of northern South America in this epoch. (One body of archaeological opinion holds that the Ostionoid culture in fact evolved directly out of the Igneri culture in Puerto Rico.) The Ostionoids would, over time, evolve a complex economic and social structure which began to take final form in about the Eleventh Century A.D., a culture known as the Taino (also often referred to as the Arawak).

This Ostionoid-Taino society (hereafter referred to simply as the Taino) differed from the earlier two cultures in many aspects, but one in particular was fundamental: their economy was based on a developed agriculture, involving the cultivation of a number of native New World plants, including cassava, peanuts, peppers, and cotton. What seems a simple, but is nonetheless an enormously consequential difference, meant that the Tainos could be a non-nomadic people, able to remain indefinitely in one site, and therefore able to build permanent villages. (At Tibes, just north of Ponce, there is an extensive recreation of such a village, adjacent to a complex of *bateyes*, or ceremonial ball courts).

The fact that they were able to stay in one locale also gave the Tainos the opportunity to develop to a much higher level the physical, social and ideo-

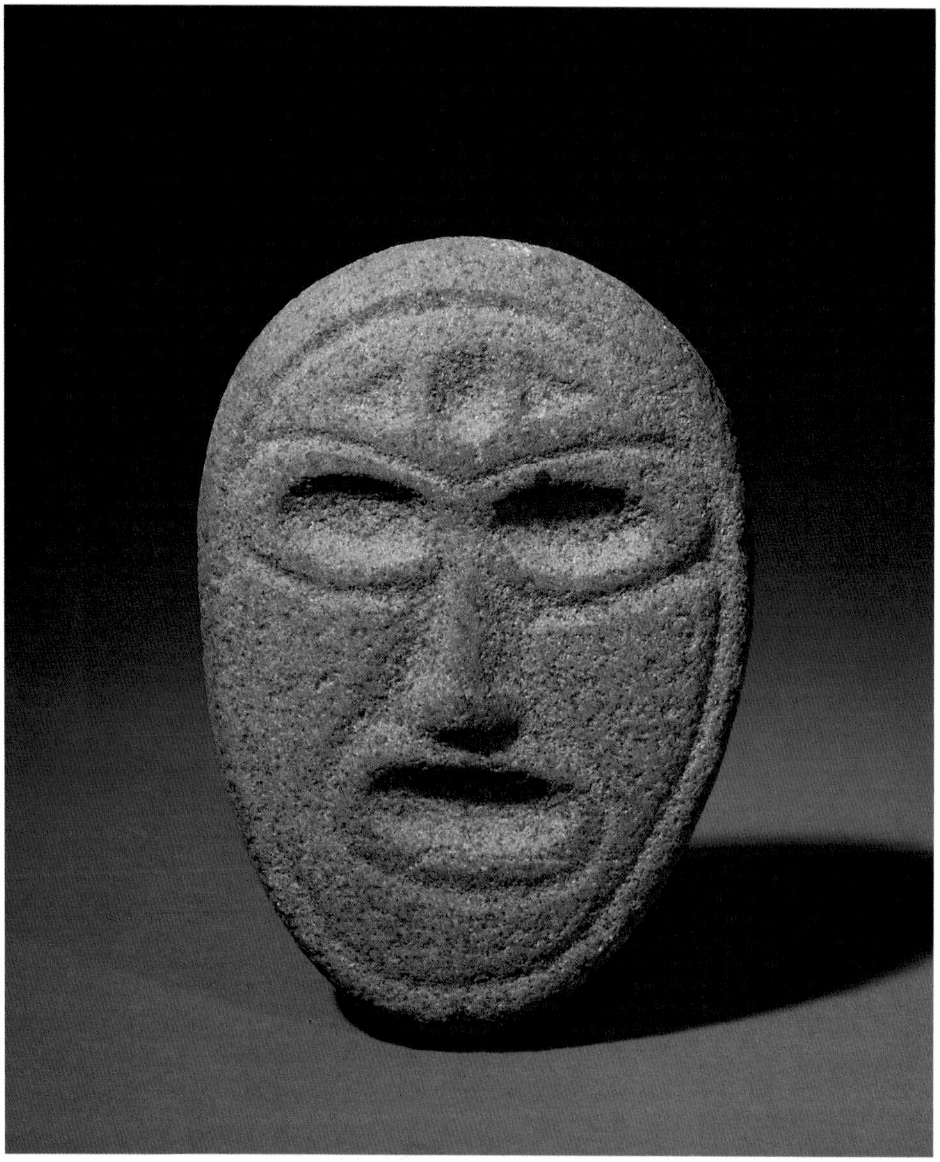

The Tainos, the last Indian culture to occupy the island, and the best documented, lived by a developed agriculture which provided the stable base for an advanced culture, reflected in the artifacts found at sites throughout the island. The most striking are zemis [this page], thought to be miniature representations of deities. The meaning of the petroglyphs (also of Taino origin, but in some cases of doubtful provenance) found at sites such as Jayuya, Caguana, and the Cueva del Indio, near Arecibo [opposite page], is less certain, although many of them may also represent Taino gods.

The Tainos traveled from island to island throughout the Caribbean in dugout canoes, some of which were far larger than the one depicted here, and capable of carrying several dozen people. The word canoe *is one of a number of words from the Taino culture which have survived into the present day, including* hurricane, hammock, *and* tobacco. *At Tibes, near Ponce [opposite page], a museum and reconstructed village bring to life the Taino world. [Print from Benzoni's* Historia del Mondo Nuovo, *1563; courtesy of the Granger Collection]*

logical aspects of their culture. Among the survivors of that latter aspect of Taino society is the *cemí*, a small idol which was fashioned of wood or stone, and usually bearing human-like features. The *cemíes* served as symbols of the Taino deities and were used in both religious rites and in everyday prayer as an aid in communicating with these gods. (Inhaling a strong tobacco mixture helped the Tainos achieve a mental state conducive to such communication).

Undoubtedly the most elaborate evidence of the Tainos' advanced socio-religious development, however, are the *bateyes* (ceremonial ball courts) where the Tainos performed religious celebrations called *areytos* as well as a ball game (which probably resembled a rough version of modern soccer). The largest and most developed complex of ball courts found in Puerto Rico, or anywhere, for that matter, is in the Cordillera Central at Caguana, near Utuado. Extensively restored in the early 1950s, the Caguana courts date from about the 12th Century, and many of the courts are surrounded by a row of upright stones bearing petroglyphs.

The Tainos had inhabited *Boriquén*, as they called their island, for over eight hundred years when they began facing a threat from another culture which had, for some time, been making its way up the Lesser Antilles from Venezuela. It was primarily a nomadic, hunting-based culture, and two of the characteristics of the prehistoric hunting cultures were their aggressivity and their need for a large expanse of territory for survival (compared to the greater land-efficiency of the agricultural societies such as the Taino). As a successful culture, with an expanding population, the Caribs, as they are known, were continually in need of new territory, and as the century drew to a close the struggle for *Boriquén* was about to begin in earnest. (The

Christoforo Colombo (Christopher Columbus to the English-speaking world, Cristóbal Colón to the Spanish) born in 1451 to a family of cloth weavers, and apprenticed to the same trade, nonetheless turned to the great seafaring tradition of his native city-state, Genoa, in today's Italy. Chance and historical circumstance pointed him westward, and he became obsessed with proving the fastest way to the spice-rich "Indies" (now part of Indonesia) lay in sailing to the west, around the earth.

After years of attempts, Columbus had finally succeeded in persuading King Ferdinand and Queen Isabella of Spain to support his Indies project. On the 17th of April, 1492, Their Catholic Majesties signed the agreement under which Columbus would sail westward across the uncharted Atlantic in search of the East. [Both prints: the Granger Collection]

name lives on to this day, slightly modified, as *Borinquen*, the popular traditional name for Puerto Rico. Other Taino words have survived into the modern era, such as hammock, canoe, tobacco, and hurricane, and in the names of island towns such as Caguas, Jayuya, and Utuado. The name of this fierce Indian tribe at war with the Tainos, the *Caribs*, has of course survived in the name of the surrounding sea and region.)

That struggle for *Borinquen* would, indeed, occur, but not with the Caribs. Rather, the struggle would be with another society altogether, a culture so far removed from the Taino experience that the Taino would not at first even realize that these new arrivals were even mortals, just ordinary human beings like themselves. And when they did at last come to this belated realization, the battle was already lost, for the society from which these white men sprung had long before won the battle on the field of technology.

Thousands of miles to the east, on a continent as far removed in time as it was in distance, a continent doubtless even beyond the imagination of the peoples of the island eden, another culture, driven by expanding commercial interests and an expanding concept of nationalism, was aggressively testing the limits of its known world. On the southwestern tip of that continent, where Europe juts farthest out into the Atlantic, it was the Portuguese who in the 1400s had pushed farthest into that vast ocean. Inspired, coaxed, and encouraged by Prince Henry ("Henry the Navigator"), fourth son of King John I, the Portuguese were driving their ships ever farther south along the coast of Africa, with the thought of rounding that huge, unknown, "dark" continent and sailing to the riches of the East.

Those great riches—both real and imaginary—of China, Japan, and the "Indies" had been known and dreamed of for centuries. The stories of the travels of the Venetian Marco Polo and his family to China in the late 13th Century had confirmed the wealth that awaited those who could find an economical sea route to Cathay (China), Cipangu (Japan), and the Spice Islands.

No one was more captivated by the dream of reaching those legendary lands than a Genoan born at mid-century to a family of weavers, and christened with his Italian name, Christoforo Colombo. Although apprenticed to his family trade, by the time he was in his teens he had already tasted the life of the seaman, and it was on the sea that he would seek his fortune.

The turning point in that fortune came in 1476, when as a crewman on a voyage from Genoa to Belgium he was shipwrecked off Portugal. With several of his shipmates he managed to reach shore and journeyed to Lisbon, and over the next several years Portugal became his adopted home. It was during this time, too, that Colombo (or Columbus, as he is known to the English-speaking world) began to form the idea—perhaps obsession would be a better word—of reaching the East by sailing westward and circumnavigating the earth.

In 1484 Columbus approached the King of Portugal, John II, with his plan. The fundamental concept on which his scheme was based—that the earth was round—was not, contrary to myth, revolutionary; that was, in fact, accepted theory among educated people of the day. It was rather Columbus's estimate of the size of the earth (and therefore the length of the voyage westward) which was novel. His plan was rejected by King John's advisors, who believed (correctly, as it turned out) the earth considerably larger, and that a westward voyage to reach the Indies would therefore be beyond the non-stop endurance of any ship of the day.

Rebuffed by the Portuguese, in the following year Columbus departed Portugal and moved with his idea to Spain. His timing was inauspicious: in 1485 and for another eight years thereafter the Spanish were engaged in the struggle to complete the ouster of the Moors from the country. When he did manage to gain an audience with the Spanish monarchs, they turned him down, despite

On August 3, 1492, Columbus set sail from the port of Palos in southern Spain with 87 men, in the Santa María, *the* Pinta *and the* Niña, *and sailed toward the dawn of a new world. (The depiction of the presence of Ferdinand and Isabella at Palos in this romanticized painting is mythical. Print: the Granger Collection.)*

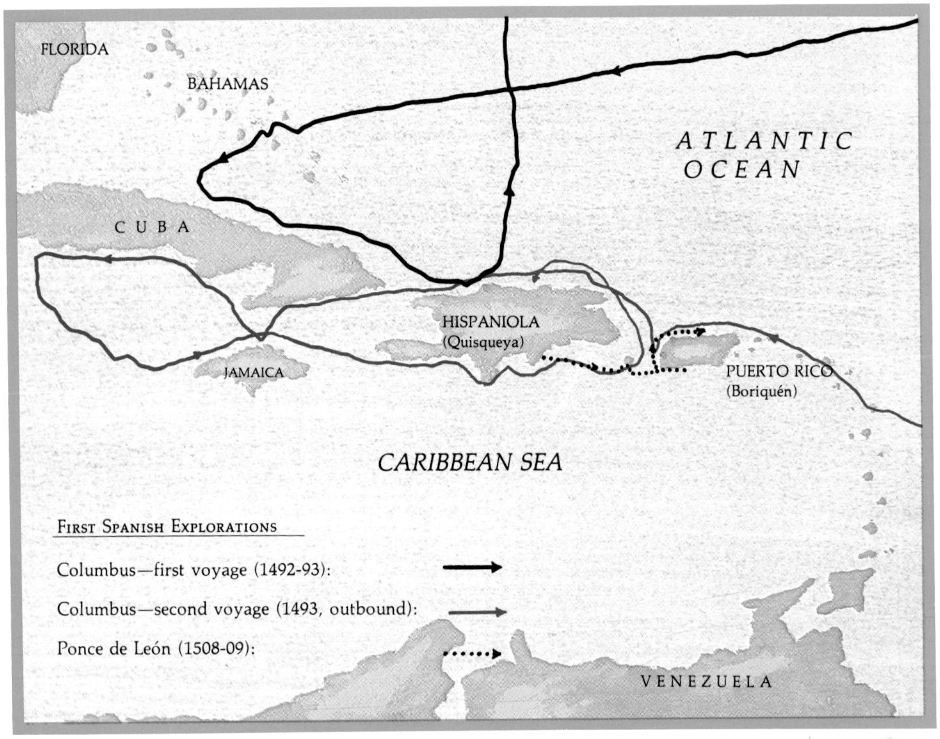

After sailing westward for ten weeks, on the morning of October 12 Columbus and his crew sighted an island in the Bahamas called Guanahaní by the Indians, which Columbus dubbed San Salvador.

On his second voyage to the New World, Columbus discovered Puerto Rico on November 19, 1493, naming it San Juan Bautista in honor of the royal heir. The expedition came ashore for two days on the west coast before hurrying on to Hispaniola (this marked the only time Columbus trod what is today American soil). [Print: the Granger Collection]

being intrigued by his scheme. Over the course of the next eight years Columbus, or Cristóbal Colón, as he now called himself, pursued his dream, scratching out a living as a sailor, map maker, and with the aid of a small stipend from the Spanish Crown. While continuing his attempts to persuade Ferdinand and Isabella, he also approached, unsuccessfully, the English and French monarchs.

Finally, in the spring of 1492, their Catholic Majesties, fresh from their victory over the Moors, agreed to sponsor Columbus's plan. At long last, after years of dreaming, struggle, and disappointment—years in which he would pass from young manhood into middle age—he would sail west to his destiny.

On August 3, just after sunrise, he left the port of Palos in southern Spain with a crew of about 90 men. After a brief stop in the Canary Islands, the three little ships known to schoolchildren the world over, the *Santa María* (his flagship), the *Pinta*, and the *Niña*, sailed westward into the uncharted Atlantic on the 8th of September. Thirty-three days later, just before dawn on the 12th of October, a lookout on the *Pinta* sighted land—an island in the Bahamas called by the Indians Guanahaní. (That October morning was, as is written on the impressive monument to Columbus's great voyage in the Plaza de Colón in Madrid, the dawn of the New World. But for Columbus, it was the moment of the fulfillment of his dream of reaching the "Indies" by sailing westward, the crowning moment of his life. By all evidence he carried with him to his death the conviction that the lands he had found were a part of Asia, and to this day, in testament to his conviction, the islands of the Caribbean are known as the West Indies.)

It was on the Great Admiral's second voyage, in 1493 (he would eventually make a total of four

El Adelantado IUAN PONCE Des=
cubridor de la Florida.

Founder and first governor of the colony, Ponce de León holds the place of honor in San Juan's Plaza de San José. For fifteen years after Puerto Rico's discovery the Spanish, busy with other explorations and their colony on neighboring Hispaniola, ignored the island. Then in the summer of 1508 Juan Ponce de León set out from Hispaniola with a force of 50 men to colonize Puerto Rico, which he would oversee as governor in its crucial formative years.

In 1512, Ponce de León would undertake an expedition leading to the discovery of Florida, before returning to Puerto Rico; during his second expedition to Florida in 1521 he would be fatally wounded in an Indian attack. [Print of Ponce de León courtesy of the Granger Collection]

voyages to the New World), that he sighted and landed on *Boriquén*, naming it San Juan Bautista, ("Saint John the Baptist"), in honor of both the saint and the son of the Spanish sovereigns. (In the 1500s, through common usage, the name bestowed upon the principal city, "Puerto Rico"—meaning rich, or exquisite, port—and that given to the island, were exchanged for each other.) But Columbus was already sufficiently burdened with the tasks of establishing the colony in nearby Santo Domingo and continuing his explorations to tarry long. His stop was only long enough to reprovision and claim the island for Spain, and after a stay of two days he hurried on to Hispaniola, leaving *Boriquén* and its overawed Taino population to wonder at this incredible development in a theretofore unchanging existence.

Some fifteen years would pass, with the Tainos having no further knowledge of these godlike creatures save what they might have learned from any kinsmen from Hispaniola. If they did learn of the Spaniards' activities on neighboring *Quisqueya* (the Indian name for Hispaniola), it could not have been encouraging: for despite some efforts led by Catholic priests to protect them, the Tainos suffered greatly under the Spanish occupation. In need of manual labor to work their gold mines and farms, and, as aspiring gentlemen and people of position, being disinclined to perform such work themselves, the Spanish pressed the Indians into service. Unused to slave labor conditions, and exposed for the first time to European diseases for which they had no immunity, the Taino population was being rapidly decimated.

In 1508, Juan Ponce de León, who had accompanied Columbus as a soldier on his second, colonizing voyage (in which some 1500 men and 17 ships, had taken part), and who had later returned to Hispaniola to live, was given the task of colonizing Puerto Rico. He arrived on August 12 of that year with a force of 50 men, landing on the south coast. After exploring the island and discovering a magnificent bay on the north coast, he ordered the colony's first settlement, Caparra, to be established some two miles south of it.

Named governor of the colony the following year, Ponce de León would oversee the colony's first, crucial years; but in 1512, lured by the promise of a fountain with miraculous curative powers, a veritable "fountain of youth," he departed on the voyage which would lead him to the discovery of Florida. (On a second voyage there in 1521 he would be mortally wounded in an Indian skirmish, later to die in Havana. In the mid-16th Century his remains were brought back to Puerto Rico to be permanently interred.)

For the European settlers of Puerto Rico and their eventual descendants, that August day in 1508 would mark a historic beginning. But for the Tainos, alas, it was the beginning of the end: for precisely the same pattern of enslavement, overwork, and death by disease which had been set in Hispaniola would evolve in Puerto Rico, and by the late 1500s the Indian population as an ethnic group had disappeared, although through extensive intermarriage with the Spanish and African populations the Taino became a permanent part of the island's racial heritage.

Outpost of Empire

The colony would grow slowly in its early years, for, as has been mentioned, the Spanish were busy in other areas of their new realm, and deposits of gold, eagerly sought and soon found, soon proved to be very limited, and the early Spaniards in the New World were not inclined to remain long in a place where there were not good prospects of finding a fortune in precious metal. Nonetheless by 1521 a town of some 300 settlers was beginning to take shape on the small island on the northern side of San Juan Bay (the initial settlement to the south of the bay, at Caparra, had been abandoned after a few years when it became apparent that the open and marshy terrain made the site ideal both for insect propagation and Indian attacks). Although, as has been mentioned, Juan Ponce de León had left in search of fortune and the "Fountain of Youth" in Florida, his family in 1521 began the construction of a stone house which would become the finest dwelling in the town. (With numerous modification and renovations it survives to this day, and was, until its recent conversion to a museum, the oldest continuously inhabited dwelling in the New World, offering both a superb view of San Juan Bay as well as a glimpse of how a prosperous family of the colonial gentility lived in the 16th and 17th Centuries.)

By 1530 the colony still numbered less than 600 white settlers (and some 2000 African slaves), and while the majority continued to reside in or near San Juan, efforts were going forward to settle other areas of the island as well. A town had been established on Guánica Bay as early as 1510, but was soon abandoned; a similar fate befell a settlement on the west coast at Aguada in the following year. In 1512 another settlement, San Germán, was also established on the west coast, but its nearness to the sea made it the frequent target of pirate attacks; in 1570 it was moved to a hilly site inland, where it has remained ever since, and thus rightly and proudly lays claim to being the second-oldest settlement on the island.

Other towns or settlements established during the 1500s included Coamo, Arecibo, and Aguada, but by 1590 the European population still numbered only a mere 2500 people. The colony's population growth was, of course, hampered by hardships such as epidemics and attacks by both Indians

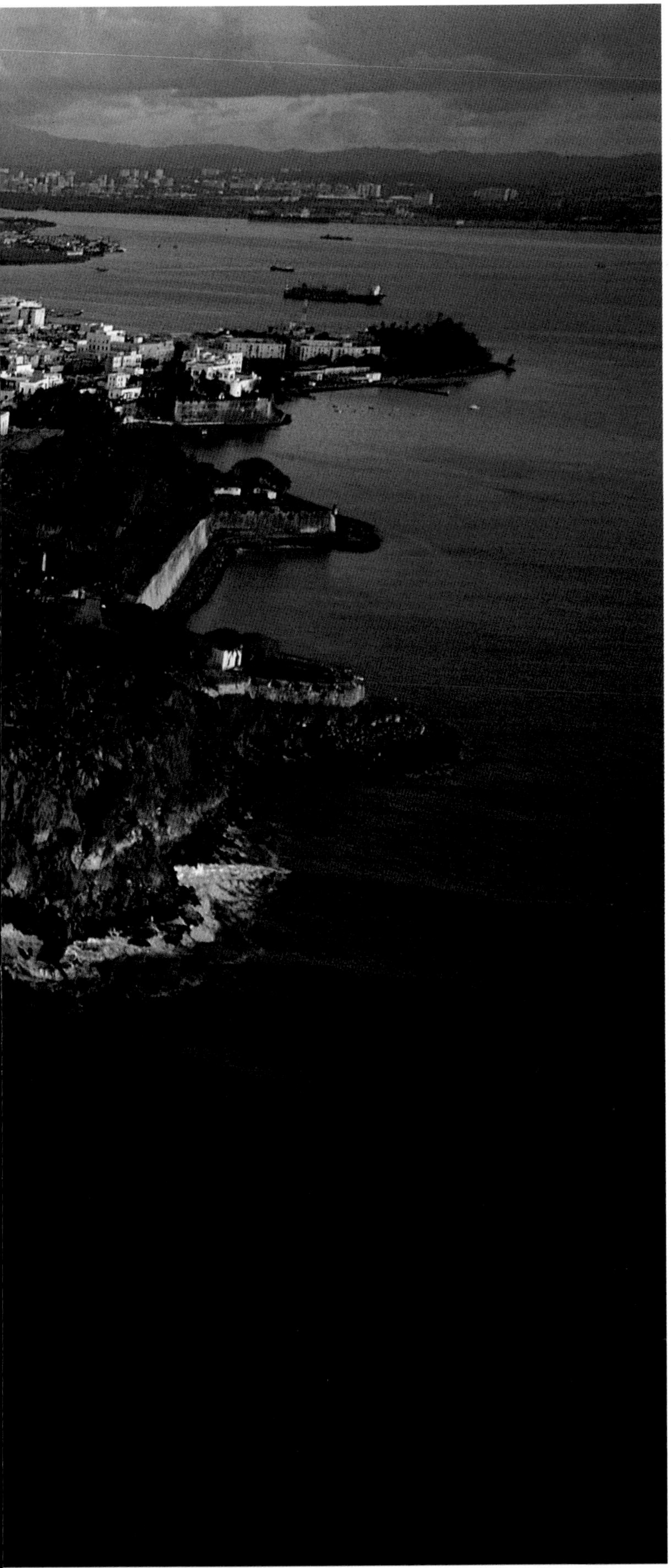

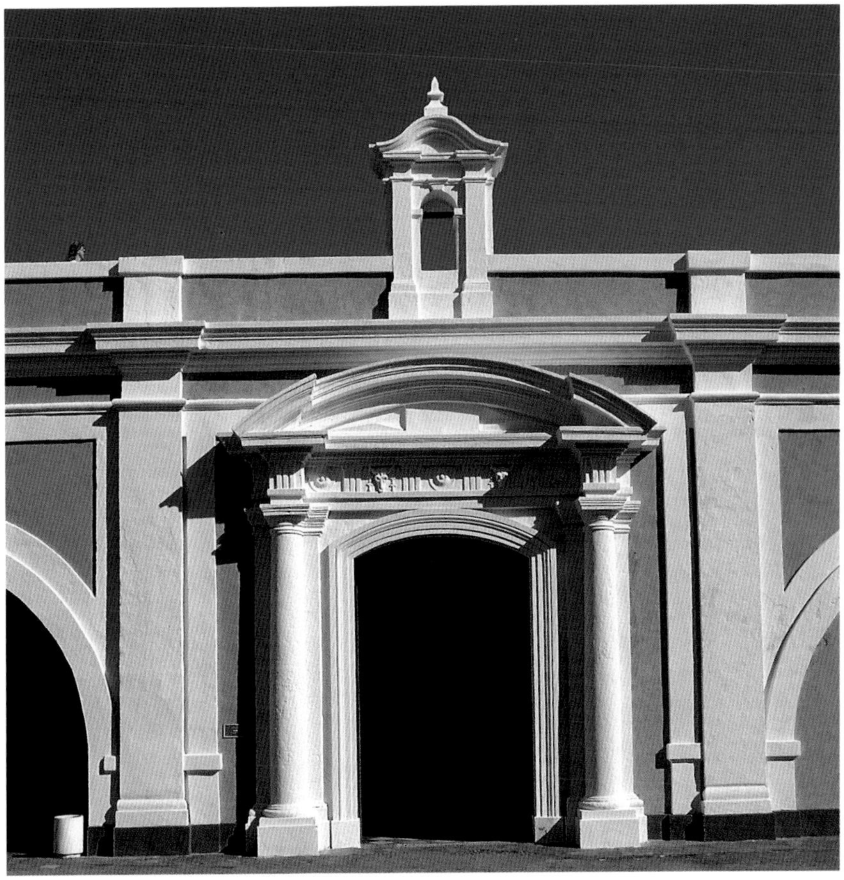

When rich deposits of gold and silver were found on the American continent, Spain's New World empire grew in importance—and so did the threat to that empire from her European enemies. To better defend Puerto Rico, in 1539 the Spanish government began building San Felipe del Morro on the headland at the eastern edge of the entrance to San Juan Bay. Toward the end of the 16th Century English and French raiders were attacking throughout the Caribbean, and in 1589 Spain began additions to El Morro which gave it the citadel form seen today, rising 140 above the sea.

As was true of all large fortifications of the day, El Morro was admirably self-contained, complete with cisterns, storerooms, sleeping quarters, and chapel [above], so as to be able to withstand an extended siege. Today El Morro forms part of the San Juan National Historic Site, administered by the U.S. Department of the Interior.

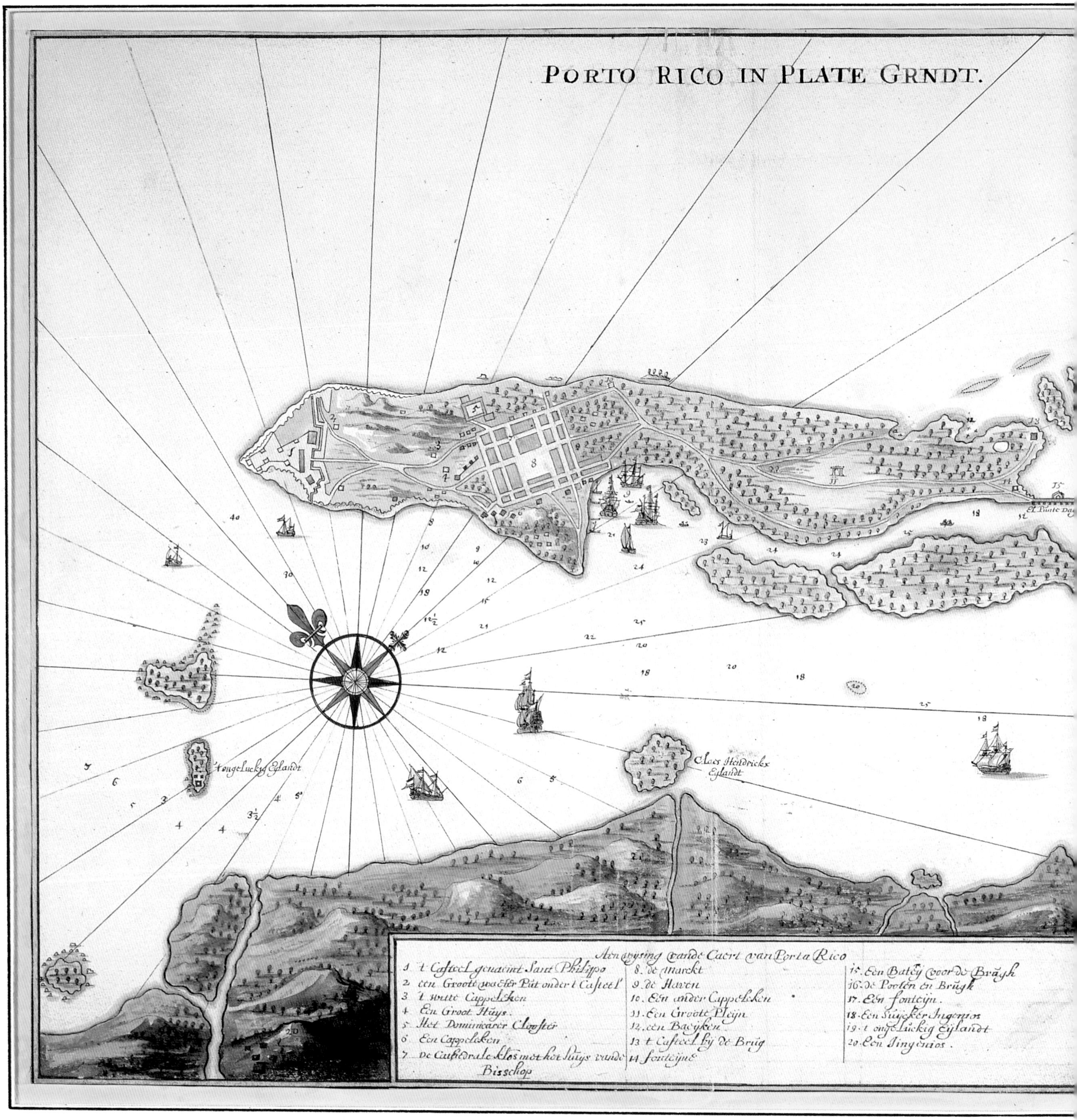
PORTO RICO IN PLATE GRNDT.
Claes Hendrickx Eylandt
Aenwysing vande Caert van Porta Rico
1 t Casteel genaemt Sant Philippo
2 een Groote water Put onder t Casteel
3 t witte Cappelleken
4 Een Groot Huys.
5 Het Dominicaner Clooster
6 Een Cappeleken
7 De Cathedrale kloos met het Huys vande Bisschop
8. de Marckt
9. de Haven
10. Een ander Cappeleken
11. Een Groote Pleyn
12. een Baeyken
13 t Casteel bij de Brug
14 fonteyne
15. Een Batey voor de Brugh
16. de Poolen en Brugh
17. Een fonteyn.
18. Een Suycker Ingenios
19. t ongelückig Eylandt
20. Een Ingenios.

San Juan, circa 1625. [From the Atlas Mayor *of Johannes Vingboons (Amsterdam, 1670); prints courtesy of the Netherlands State Archives]*

and pirates, but perhaps the most significant impediment to growth during this period was the arrival of the news of the fabulous wealth discovered by Pizarro in Peru. "May God take me to Peru!" became the cry in the 1530s, and for a time the colony's population actually decreased due to emigration to the other Spanish colonies. (In fact, so serious was the threat to the colony's very existence that the Spanish authorities declared severe penalties for unauthorized departures.)

But despite the settlements out on the island, it was above all San Juan which commanded the primary attention of the Spanish authorities, for the reason which has already been alluded to: with the development of Spain's vastly larger colonies both on the American continents and in the rest of the Caribbean, and with the beginning of regular shipments of gold and silver from those colonies back to the mother country, the need for the protection of those ocean shipments became vital. A glance at a map, and an understanding of the prevailing winds which dictated the route of square rigged sailing vessels (northeast from Havana, then through the Bahamas Strait and eastward across the Atlantic) shows why: although Puerto Rico is not directly on that route, had the island fallen into unfriendly hands the task of protecting those annual treasure convoys would have been greatly complicated. Thus possession of Puerto Rico was vital to the Spanish, and San Juan and its strategic bay were the key element in maintaining control of the island.

So the Spanish crown began construction of the forts and walls which would eventually ensure the city's defense: the first, begun in 1537, was the palace-fortress which came to be called, simply enough, *La Fortaleza,* meaning "the Fortress." (Casa Blanca, the house built by the Ponce de León family, was at times used as a stronghold against Indian attacks, but it had been built primarily as a residence.) Its location was apparently chosen with an eye to ease of access for arriving ships; unfortunately, that location was not the logical choice for the best defense of the harbor, and it soon became apparent that a stronger fort on El Morro ("The Headland"), dominating the harbor entrance, was indicated. In 1539 construction of that fort, which would be named San Felipe del Morro, was authorized, to be financed from the treasury of the Vice-Royalty of Mexico, a subsidy which would continue to be the main financial support of the island's government until the Mexican revolt early in the 19th Century.

Repeated pirate attacks at various points on the island during the 16th Century, and especially the attacks by Drake in 1595, the Earl of Cumberland in 1598 (the latter succeeding in occupying El Morro for a period of some weeks), and the Dutch in 1625, made it evident that stronger fortifications were needed to protect the city and its population from landward attack, and therefore in about 1634 construction began on Fort San Cristóbal and the walls of the city.

San Cristóbal remains today, a magnificent example of European defense construction of the 17th and 18th Centuries (and, since 1949, a National Historic Site administered by the National Park Service), and perhaps the island's most visible reminder of the principal role Puerto Rico was to play on the world scene for the more than two centuries immediately following the fort's construction.

The fact that the Spanish early on came to look at Puerto Rico primarily as a strategic location, of value principally for its role in guarding the sea lanes to other colonies, would be crucial to its development; which is to say, the resources and attitude accorded to it by the Crown. In the early 17th Century, the Spanish were suffering an embarrassment of riches: Spain had discovered and claimed for itself an expanse of territory in the New World many times larger than Spain itself, an expanse so vast that its full extent would not even be fully realized until well into the 19th Century. Some of these territories, particularly Mexico and Peru, were proving fabulously rich in gold and silver, while others had vast potential for agricultural development. Spain simply had not

As was the case with the most important of Spain's colonial outposts, San Juan was defended by a massive stone wall encircling the city. The wall on the southern and eastern sides was torn down in 1897 to make room for the expansion of the city, but the wall still exists on the northern and western sides, and is anchored at its northeastern corner by Fort San Cristóbal. Both the wall and the immense fort were begun about 1634 to defend against land attack on the city, and to this day San Cristóbal dominates Plaza Colón and the eastern approach to Old San Juan.

Together with its fortifications, San Juan's oldest buildings are its religious structures: bordering the Plaza de San José on the north is the oldest church building in Puerto Rico (and the second oldest in the New World), the Church of San José [opposite page], which dates from the 1530s.

Next to it, the Convento de los Domínicos [this page] also dates from the 16th Century. (As is the case with virtually all of the island's buildings of the 16th and 17th Centuries, both have been extensively modified and restored over the years.)

enough men, money and resources—ships, arms, tools, the whole gamut of materials needed—to be able to establish and maintain all of these new colonies.

Faced with this situation, Spain naturally and logically concentrated its resources where the payoff would be greatest. Puerto Rico, lacking in precious metals and tiny alongside the other Spanish colonies, was simply passed by in the rush to richer prizes (even neighboring Hispaniola, not much larger when considered against the immensity of the continents, nonetheless received far more attention and resources, as the first seat of government for Spain's New World possessions).

There have been, through the years, various definitions of a colony, but one concept is central to the classic definition: a colony exists for the benefit of the mother country. Thus Puerto Rico, much too small and without metallic wealth, was unable to command Spanish attention to developing it, and simply languished during most of the 17th and 18th, and even into the 19th Centuries. There were some developments during this period, of course: new towns were settled; by 1750 some 14 had been founded. By the end of that century another 25 towns, including Ponce, Mayagüez, Fajardo, and Humacao, had been started. The island's population, still only 45,000 in 1765, would triple to over 150,000 in 1800, as the steadily improving agricultural picture continued to attract new immigrants. The early development of the sugar industry in the 16th Century proved short-lived, however, unable to compete with the more advanced technology of the English and French sugar colonies. Cattle (hides), ginger and tobacco would take its place; then in the mid-18th Century coffee would be introduced, drawing a sizeable population to the mountainous interior for the first time, and becoming the leading export of the 19th Century.

The island's development was also hampered in this period by Spain's mercantilist trade policies, which restricted colonial commerce to the mother country alone; nonetheless, so stretched were her shipping resources—and so active the pirates in the Caribbean—that periods of years could, and did, pass without a single Spanish commercial vessel calling at the island. In this environment, not surprisingly, smuggling flourished.

The trade monopoly was lifted in 1815, part of a Spanish response to growing agitation in the New World for a "fairer deal," as we might put it today. Philosophies and attitudes toward royal authority were undergoing a sea change all over the world, and the Americas were at the forefront of this shift. The revolt of the thirteen English colonies, and later, of the Spanish colonies, were of course among the most far-reaching expressions of this profound ideological evolution.

In Puerto Rico these winds of change were felt as well, although, given the size of the colony and the make-up of the population (the island had acquired many pro-Royalists from other, rebelling, Spanish colonies), they were somewhat muted. Nonetheless, during the course of the 19th Century sentiment and agitation grew for an easing of the harshness of Spanish rule, and the granting of civil and political rights to the colony. The mood for change took two primary courses: the first called for separation, that is, independence, from Spain; the second, though demanding political and civil liberties identical to those enjoyed in the mother country, sought local self-rule without separation, or autonomy.

The first movement, whose principal leader was a physician named Ramón E. Betances, reached its apogee in 1868 when a small band of separatist sympathizers mounted a revolt in Lares, at the northern edge of the coffee country. Quickly put down the following day, the revolt had no lasting military consequences, and in fact was the only native challenge of arms ever made against Spanish rule during the island's history. But during their brief moment of glory the would-be revolu-

Centerpiece of Calle Cristo, the Cathedral of San Juan Bautista. The first church on the site was erected in 1521, the year the city was founded. That early rustic church was destroyed by hurricane in 1539; the present structure dates from the early 1800s, and contains the tomb of the colony's founder, Ponce de León.

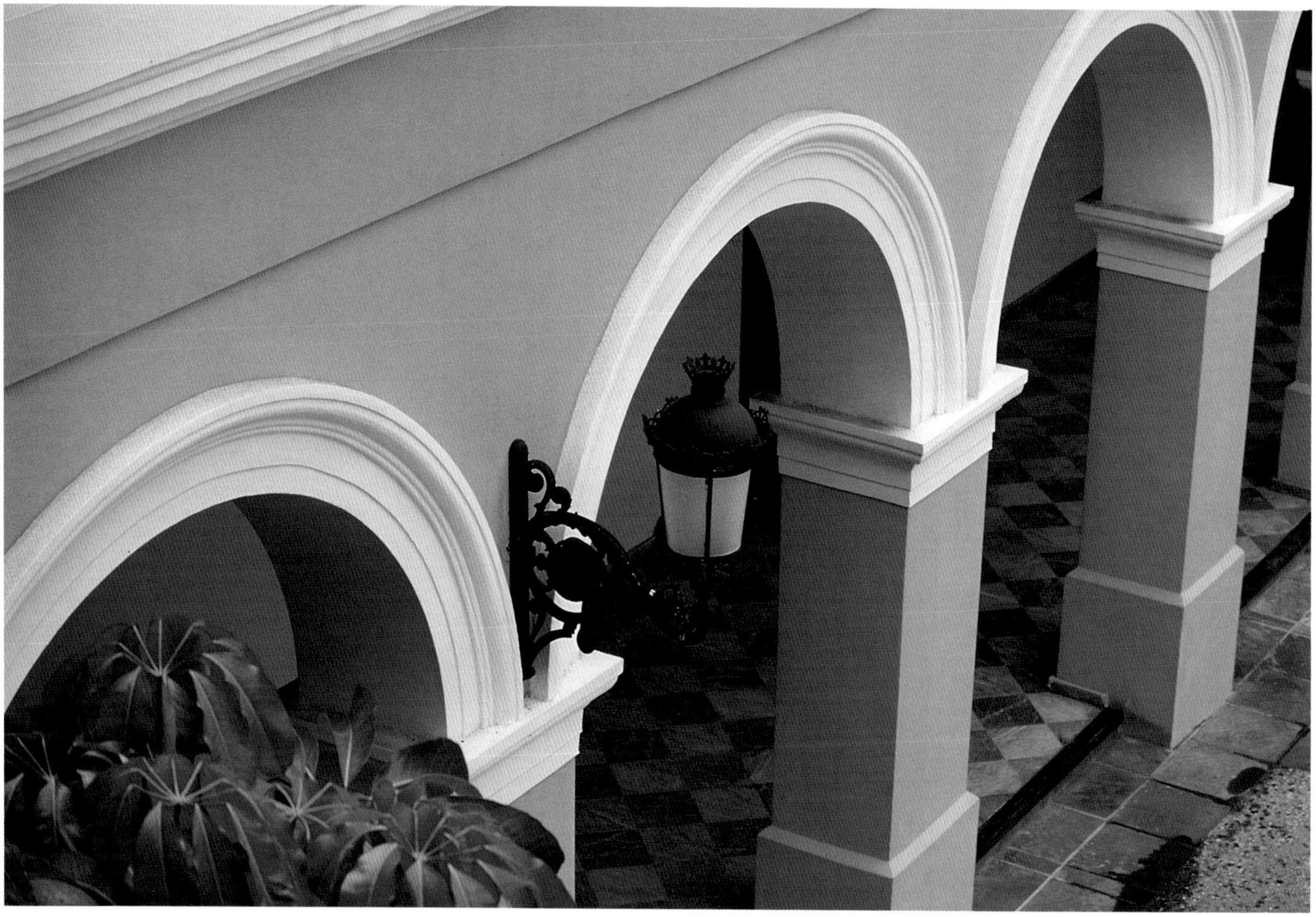

For the first three centuries of its existence Puerto Rico remained a backwater of the Spanish Empire, but the loss of her South American possessions and the island's growing autonomist sentiments focussed Spain's mind on her remaining colonies. Thus during the 19th Century the Crown multiplied its investment in the island. Two architectural gems which resulted, recently restored for use as offices of the Commonwealth government, are the Real Intendencia [this page], at the west end of the Plaza de Armas, and the offices of the Department of Foreign Relations on Calle Fortaleza [opposite page].

With the rapid population growth of the 1800s came the invasion of the mountainous interior, and with it, the birth of the jíbaro, *the hardy people of the highlands who came to symbolize the soul of the country [here romanticized in* El Velorio *("The Wake"), by Puerto Rico's famed 19th-Century impressionist Francisco Oller. Painting: the Museum of the University of Puerto Rico].*

With the 19th Century came also a boom in coffee production and the rise of the haciendas, *where many of the* jíbaros *were employed. As government-issued money was often in short supply, the hacienda workers were usually paid in* riles *issued by the hacienda itself, which were used by the workers to make purchases at the plantation store [opposite page]. [*Riles *courtesy of the Banco Popular, posed at Hacienda Buena Vista, courtesy of the Fideicomiso de Conservación de Puerto Rico]*

LARES
JAB

The island's population remained tiny for the first two hundred years of the colony's existence (as of 1700 there were still only 7500 residents spread among eight towns, including San Juan), then began to expand rapidly from the mid-1700s. Essential to the founding of each town was its Catholic church, and to this day the Catholic church on the main plaza is the architectural pride and joy of many a town. Among the most beautiful is the famous San Antonio de Padua in Guayama, founded in 1736 [opposite page], and the recently restored Nuestra Señora del Carmen in Hatillo, on the north coast, founded in 1823 [this page].

During the 1800s San Juan filled in the area within the city walls and took on the aspect recognizable today [on this page, a view of Calle Tetuan circa 1898]. But even though the population of the island expanded from approximately 150,000 in 1800 to nearly a million at the turn of the century, San Juan remained a relatively small city, counting only some 32,000 residents in 1899.

La Marina, San Juan, Porto Rico. Custom House on Right. Naval Station Next.

The reason for San Juan's lack of growth was quite simple: at the close of the 19th Century the island remained largely rural and agricultural, and in 1899 there were no more than 175 miles of paved roads. Sugar, coffee, and tobacco exports were shipped from ports such as Ponce, Mayagüez, Fajardo, and Aguadilla rather than from San Juan [on this page, a view of the wharf and La Puntilla circa 1898]. [Prints courtesy of the Archivo General de Puerto Rico]

tionaries declared the Republic of Puerto Rico, and the gesture became known as *El Grito de Lares* ("The Cry of Lares").

(In the ensuing years the Grito de Lares would acquire considerable significance as an expression of Puerto Rican identity, and on its anniversary, September 23, the central plaza of the town has become the rallying-point (and the speakers' platform) for Puerto Ricans of *independentista* and *nacionalista* leanings.)

Perhaps the most significant consequence of the Grito de Lares was in the reaction to it: awakened to the possibility of revolt in yet another of its colonies, the Spanish government initiated a policy of extending broader freedoms to the island's inhabitants. But the trend was hardly a constant one, and the periodic retraction of liberties by the Mother Country only aggravated the demand for more equitable treatment, thus giving impetus to the growing autonomist movement in the later half of the 19th Century.

The autonomist movement counted a number of leaders, including Román Baldorioty de Castro and José Celso Barbosa, but the man whose name would become synonymous with the autonomy movement, to the point that he is sometimes identified as the "George Washington of Puerto Rico," was Luis Muñoz Rivera, the editor of the liberal newspaper *La Democracia*. It was he who led the autonomist party's commission to Spain in 1896, and when, the following year, the Spanish government granted the island an Autonomous Charter, it was he who emerged as the undisputed leader of the island's autonomous government.

But autonomy under the Spanish crown, so long dreamed of, so unexpectedly obtained, which promised so much for the budding sense of Puerto Rican nationhood, would be very short-lived indeed, and once again, as in 1493, Puerto Rico would be at the mercy of developments far beyond its shores.

In 1898 only two Spanish colonies—Cuba and Puerto Rico—remained in the Americas, and both were sufficiently close to be a particularly sharp pain in the side of the United States, whose naval strategies had long recognized the desirability of obtaining a naval base in the Caribbean—and, if possible, of getting the Spanish out. Further, during the 19th Century the new American nation had grown vast and powerful (and had developed along the way a convenient philosophy of "manifest destiny" to explain the filling in what seemed to some her "natural boundaries." Indeed, by the end of the century pressures were building to exercise the doctrine beyond the continent, and so bring the "benefits of American civilization to less fortunate peoples").

Modern Era

Thus, as the 19th Century drew to a close, Luis Muñoz Rivera and his fellow autonomists felt local home rule to be within their grasp, if they could continue to mount pressure on Spain. But on February 15, 1898, pressure on Spain became a moot point when the U.S. battleship *Maine* blew up under mysterious circumstances in Havana Harbor, and (with a not-so-gentle nudge from the American press) was to be the justification for the United States to launch into "a splendid little war" with Spain. With Admiral Dewey's destruction of the Spanish fleet at Manila Bay and the swift victory of the U.S. forces in Cuba (where Teddy Roosevelt and his Rough Riders had gained fame in their charge up San Juan Hill), the war was all but over; and when at daybreak on July 25, 1898 the U.S.S. *Gloucester* steamed into Guánica Bay on the southern coast there remained only seventeen days of hostilities to the Spanish-American War.

Finding themselves greatly outnumbered and out-gunned by the American invasion force of 16,000 troops, the Spanish forces offered only minimal resistance. The U.S. Army entered Ponce two days after the landing, then began its overland march toward the battle for San Juan. (The Puerto Rican populace, aware of the level of prosperity and civil liberties existing in the States, and hopeful that the American invasion meant a similar future for the island, whether as a part of the United States or as an independent nation, in general welcomed the U.S. troops.)

The battle for San Juan, however, would never take place, for on August 13, 1898 Spain and the United States signed the peace agreement ending hostilities, and San Juan was spared the destruction which a fierce assault would have entailed. (The Treaty of Paris, by which Spain formally ceded Puerto Rico to the U.S., was signed on December 10 of that same year.) The city and the island were turned over to the American commander, General John Brooke, who was to be the first American governor of Puerto Rico, on October 18. (The Spanish flag waving over the Arsenal at La Puntilla, where the last Spanish troops waited several days for a ship to transport them back to Spain, marked it as the last bit of Puerto Rico to remain under Spanish sovereignty.)

The Charter of Autonomy granted to Puerto Rico in 1897 has been the subject of extended debate over the years; opinion varies the whole gamut between the belief that it signaled a new era of self-government for the island, to the opinion that it was merely one more attempt on the part of Spain to forestall growing sentiments for independence.

Puerto Rico's history as a Spanish colony came to an abrupt halt in July of 1898 when U.S. troops [this page] landed on the south coast during the Spanish-American War. With the American flag and access to the American market came huge investment in the sugar industry, converting most of the coastal plain into a vast expanse of sugar cane fields [as on the opposite page, near Ponce]. Sugar's dominance of the economy led to decades-long dominance of political power as well. [Photograph of troops in Ponce: the National Archives]

By the mid-summer of 1898, when the American troops landed at Guánica Bay, only the first steps toward implementing the terms of the Charter had been taken; the real tests of the interpretation Spain would have given the Charter, and therefore its real significance for Puerto Rican self-government, lay ahead. But in the historical context, perhaps the most important point is this: when the American invasion occurred, making the Charter meaningless, the potential for self-government under the Charter was an unknown—but without question the men who had struggled so long and hard to achieve it had the highest expectations for self-rule.

(Following the dissolution of the Autonomous Government upon the American invasion, Luis Muñoz Rivera would continue to struggle for local self-rule and civil rights, now under the American flag; he would later serve as the island's Resident Commissioner in Washington, but would die in 1916 without having obtained the plebiscite on the questions of U.S. citizenship and the island's political status—whether independence, autonomy, or statehood—which he believed indispensable to Puerto Rico's political dignity.)

One thing is certain: when the Americans, uncertain of what to do with their new possession, and unaccustomed to the rule of colonial power, installed first a military government, and then a civilian government which provided for even less local autonomy than had been promised under the Autonomic Charter, the disillusionment of those leaders was inevitable. It was a disillusionment which would color the whole history of American involvement with Puerto Rico, and, indeed, which has ramifications into the present day.

The man who was to transform the island to such an extent that he is justly called the father of

Father of modern Puerto Rico, Luis Muñoz Marín [in the white suit, above], son of Luis Muñoz Rivera, wrought a revolutionary change in the power structure during the 1930s and '40s when he wrested control of the island's politics from entrenched sugar interests by taking a grassroots political campaign throughout the island, winning the confidence and the votes of the jíbaro. *His* Popular *Party won control of the legislature in 1940, and in 1948 Muñoz Marín became Puerto Rico's first elected Governor, a post he held until his retirement in 1964. [Photograph of Muñoz Marín from a private collection.]*

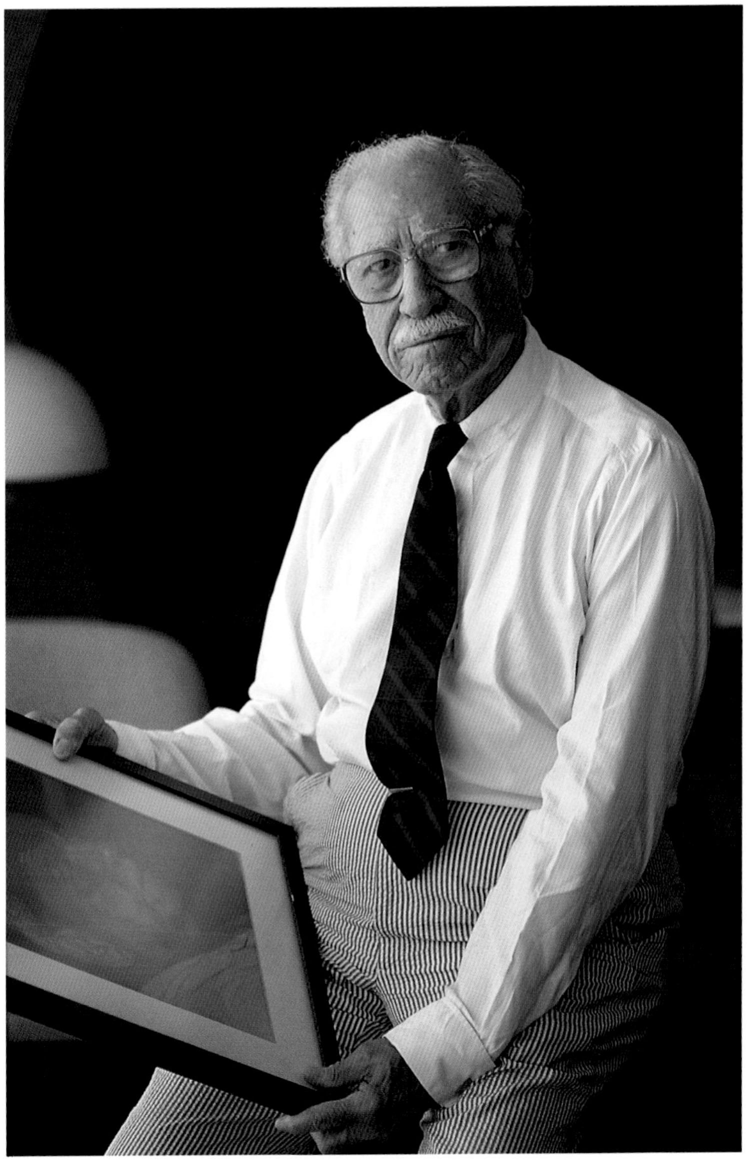

What Muñoz Marín was to Puerto Rico's politics, Teodoro Moscoso was to the island's economy: in 1942 the young pharmacist was appointed head of "Fomento," the agency charged with weaning the island's economy from its decades-long dependence on sugar production. He would go on to play key roles in promoting both tourism and cultural events, then serve as U.S. Ambassador to Venezuela and the first coordinator for John F. Kennedy's Alliance for Progress.

Until the mid-20th Century Puerto Rico remained an agricultural economy, heavily dependent on "King Sugar." Then in the 1940s the island government began a concerted drive to liberate it from its sugar monoculture. In time, "Operation Bootstrap," as the program came to be called, proved a spectacular success, attracting hundreds of companies which today employ tens of thousands of workers in the manufacturing sector. From humble beginnings in low-skill operations like sewing and textile making, the plants have steadily evolved toward "high-tech" industries, with important concentrations in pharmaceutical products [opposite page] and electronics [this page].

Magnet of the island, metropolis of the Caribbean, greater San Juan grows inexorably outward from its magnificent harbor, and today counts well over a million inhabitants, or roughly one islander in every three. (At the turn of the century the city was essentially limited to San Juan Island; today the metropolitan area, including Santurce, Carolina, Río Piedras, and Bayamón, forms a continuous urban landscape perhaps 100 times larger.)

A number of factors have contributed to this phenomenal growth: among them the mushrooming of the governmental sector, and the growing importance of the city as a transport, communications, and financial hub for the Caribbean [the banking sector is heavily concentrated in the area known as Hato Rey, above].

modern Puerto Rico, Luis Muñoz Marín, was born just months before the American invasion of 1898. Maturing with the century, he wrought a transformation of Puerto Rico's politics and economy so profound that it touched every aspect of Puerto Rican life. (At his death in May 1980 all Puerto Rico mourned, for it knew that a giant had passed from among them.)

In the early years of his life Muñoz Marín gave little outward indication of the role he was to eventually play in Puerto Rico's history. Most of his formative years were spent in the States, where he would pass his early manhood as a writer. (Although his writings were predominantly political essays or journalistic pieces, his occasional forays into poetry would earn him the nickname he was to carry all his life, *el Vate* ("the Poet").

Thus when he returned to the island to live in 1931, many of the people who had expected a great political career for Muñoz Rivera's son doubted the young man's seriousness. But even in his years away from the island the young Muñoz was gaining a perspective on Puerto Rico and its problems (indeed many of his writings had dealt with those very issues); and, perhaps equally important, on the nature and workings of the American nation, perspectives which would have been impossible to achieve from within the island. And so when Muñoz came back to Puerto Rico for good at the age of 33, he knew his own mind, and he knew what had to be done if Puerto Rico was to lose its notorious nickname, "the Poorhouse of the Caribbean."

Although America's rule over its colony had eventually established a limited democratic framework for self-rule in most local matters (the presidentially appointed governor retained a broad veto power), the rise of the great sugar interests had severely compromised the island's political processes. In the late 1930s, amidst the island's grinding poverty, it remained common for people, especially in the rural areas, to sell their votes ($5.00 or a pair of shoes was the normal price). Under these conditions, the island's government was obviously powerless to effect any change in the economic or social structure which might threaten powerful vested interests.

In 1938 Muñoz moved into this situation decisively, launching a grassroots political campaign in the countryside unlike anything Puerto Rico had ever seen. His strategy was disarmingly simple: faced with the impossible task of outbidding the entrenched economic interests in a vote-buying war, Muñoz won the *jíbaro's* confidence, and with it their votes. With the 1940 election Muñoz and his *Populares* won effective control of the island's legislature from the sugar interests, thus positioning themselves to institute their broad-ranging economic and social reforms.

With his bold political strategy, Muñoz had in the space of two years started Puerto Rico on its climb out of near-feudal conditions toward a modern, democratic society. (In the next elections four years later Muñoz and his party would consolidate their control of the legislature with an overwhelming victory; and four years after that, in 1948, Muñoz would become the first governor of the island to be elected by the Puerto Rican people. Muñoz and his *Populares* would remain in power continuously until the elections of 1968.)

Although he succeeded in lifting Puerto Rico out of the dire economic straits which had shackled the island since its beginnings, and he came to believe that Puerto Ricans would be best served under a framework of local autonomy, that is, as a "free associated state" or "commonwealth", under the American flag (a relationship which would be formalized with the adoption of the Puerto Rican Constitution in 1952), even Luis Muñoz Marín was not able to put an end to the debate which had dominated public discussion since the turn of the century: whether independence, commonwealth, or statehood would be best for the long-term interests of Puerto Rico. It is a debate which continues to rage to this day.

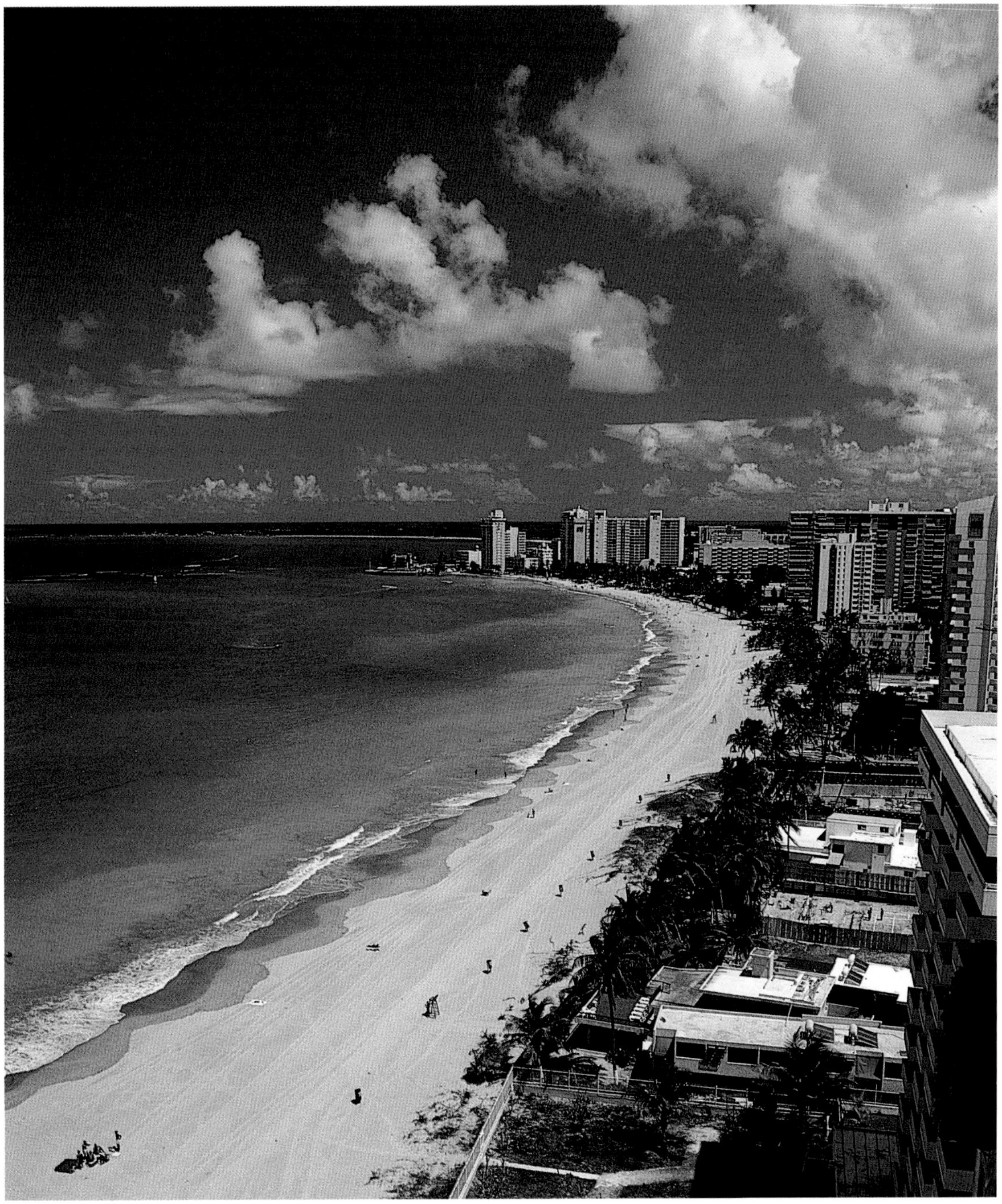

The 1950s and '60s saw the birth and growth of the mass tourism industry, with the Condado and Isla Verde areas [above, spectacular Isla Verde beach] becoming the focal point for an array of hotels and high-rise condominiums.

Mi Querido San Juan

It has now been over two decades since my first encounter with Puerto Rico and its capital. That first visit was a brief one, but I think I will never forget the sense of enchantment that descended upon me when I first saw Viejo San Juan. Discovering those lamp-lit streets of the Old City on a summer evening with a group of Peace Corps buddies was nothing short of magical. And despite my innumerable return visits to those now familiar narrow streets in the intervening years, I still retain much of the sense of wonder I felt on that initial visit those many years ago.

The San Juan I am speaking of is only a small part of the enormous San Juan metropolitan area, which counts well over a million inhabitants, or more than one in every three of the island's total; and these other areas have their attractions (including the visual, a few of which are included in this chapter). Indeed, if I were to be a permanent resident of Puerto Rico, I do not know that I would choose the Old City for my home, for I have a great fondness for greenery and open spaces. But if past experience is any guide, I would be a constant visitor, for in the many, many months I have spent on the island I doubt that more than three or four days have ever gone by without my paying a visit to my favorite haunts of the ancient part of the city.

Part of the attraction is of course professional: no one with a camera can walk a block in Old San Juan without wanting to stop to focus on a building facade, a roofline, a doorway, or a slice of life that is ever present and close to hand. (Except very late at night or on purely social occasions, I am never there without my camera bag, and on nearly every visit I am astonished at seeing things that had previously escaped my notice.)

But an equal part of the city's appeal, for me at least, is the sheer weight of history that pervades the atmosphere. It is true, as is sometimes pointed out, that by European standards, much of the city is not ancient: compared to the *vieilles villes* of Europe, many of the buildings would be thought of as modern, dating as they do from the 19th Century and later. But the core of the city traces back more than four centuries; it is older than any other city under the American flag. Some of its founders, including the first governor of the colony, Ponce de León, were contemporaries of Columbus. For a person like myself, raised in the western United States, where very little predates this century, San Juan represents a contact with the roots of our history that is rare indeed.

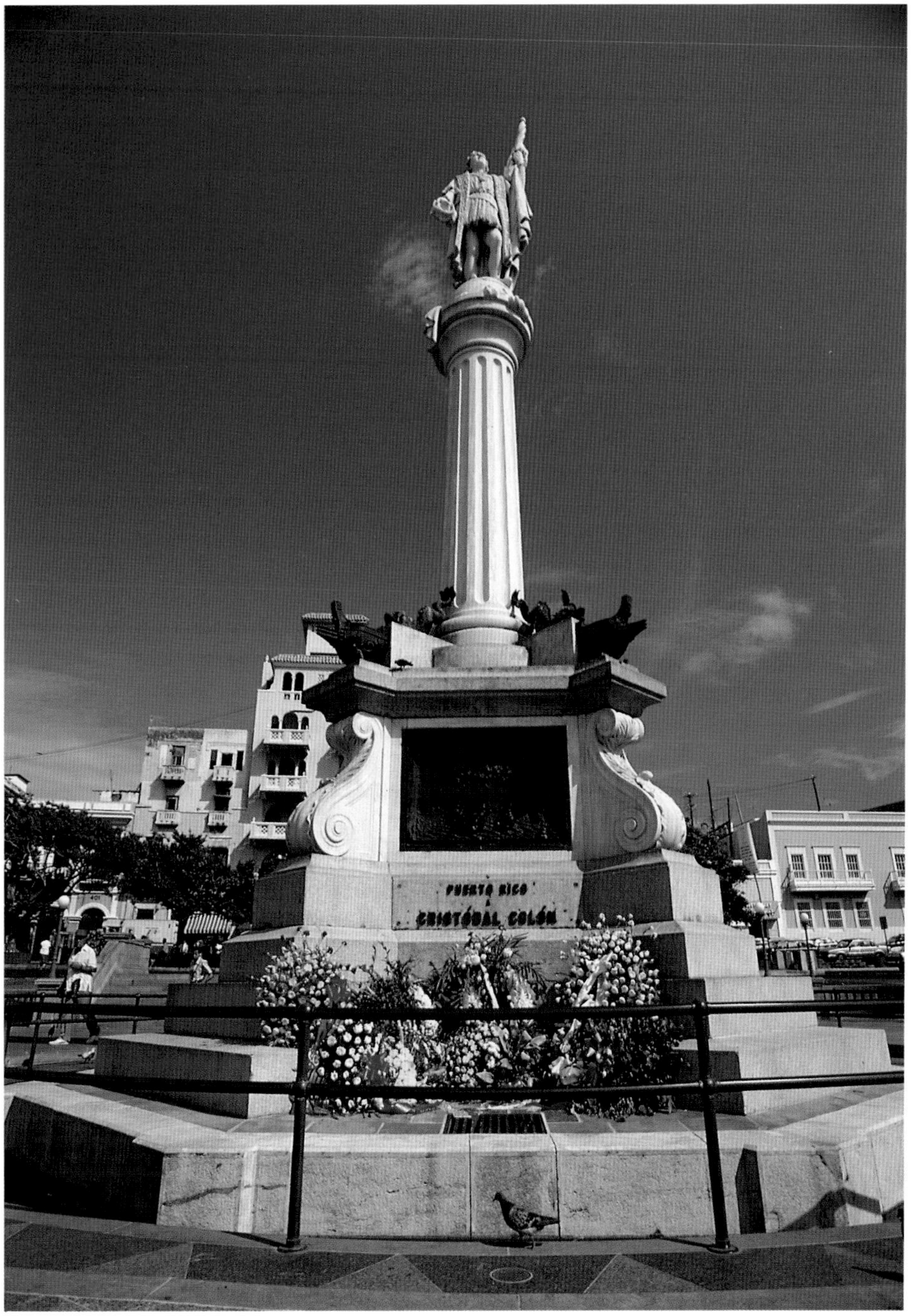

Standing high above the plaza named in his honor, Cristóbal Colón gazes over San Juan Bay and the island he discovered. Prior to the erection of the Columbus statue in 1893, the square was the Plaza de Santiago, and a statue of Ponce de León held the place of honor. (The Ponce de León statue was moved to the Plaza de San José, where it still stands.)

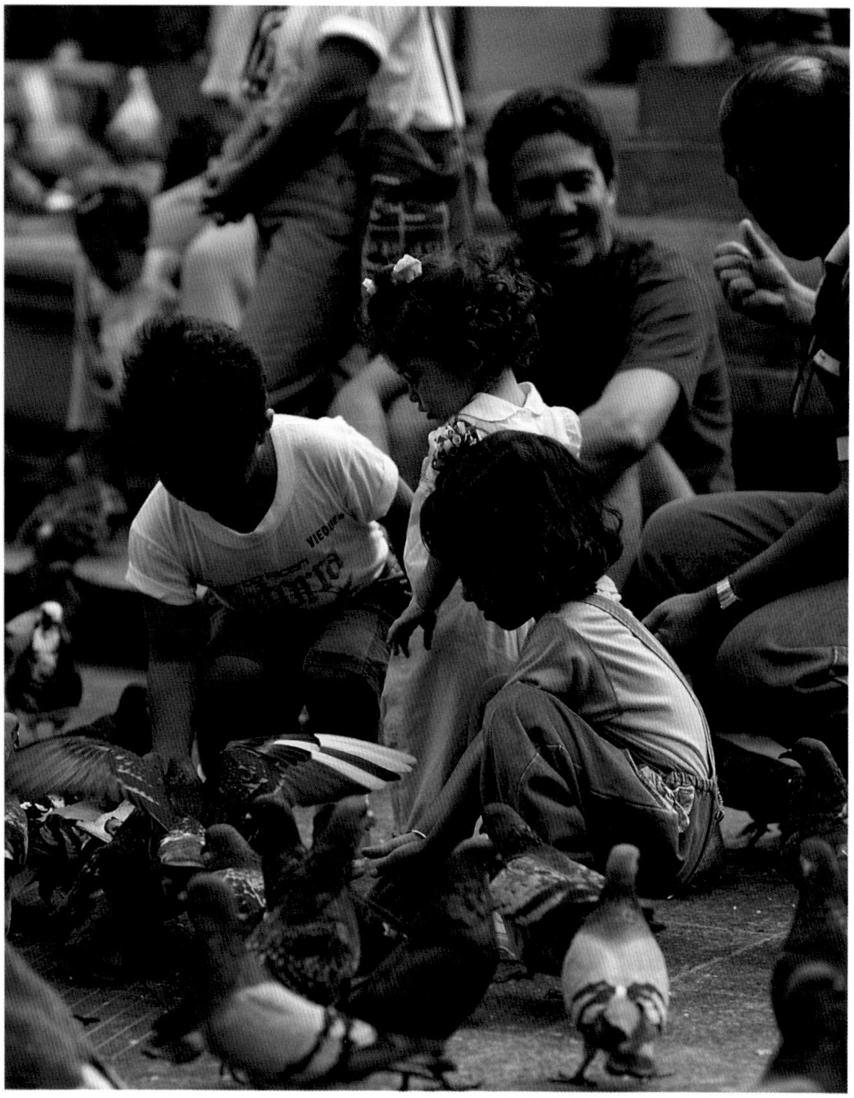

Crossroads and meeting place of Viejo San Juan, the Plaza de Armas—known variously during its history as the Plaza Mayor, the Plaza Principal, the Plaza Alfonso XII, and the Plaza de la Constitución—has been the scene of parades, speeches, demonstrations, weary tourists, running children, and pigeon feeding. The Casa Alcadía, or City Hall [opposite page], dates from 1604, and was rebuilt to its present form in 1840.

[Following spread:] Evening falls over the Plaza de Armas, sentimental heart of the city.

Two striking buildings on Avenida Ponce de León near the Plaza de Colón, both built early in this century: the Old Casino of San Juan, erected in 1917 and recently restored, now serves as the Official Government Reception Center [this page]. Founded in 1876, the Ateneo Puertorriqueño is the island's oldest cultural-promotion institution, and moved to its present building in 1922 [opposite page].

ATENEO PUERTORRIQUEÑO

The beauty of Old San Juan, the oldest European city under the American flag, lies largely in the endless variety and striking colors of its Spanish Colonial architecture, much of which dates from the 18th and 19th Centuries. After falling into a sorry state of disrepair in the early decades of this century, the city was rescued through the efforts of concerned citizens and local government, working under the guidance of the Institute for Puerto Rican Culture and its first director, Dr. Ricardo Alegría.

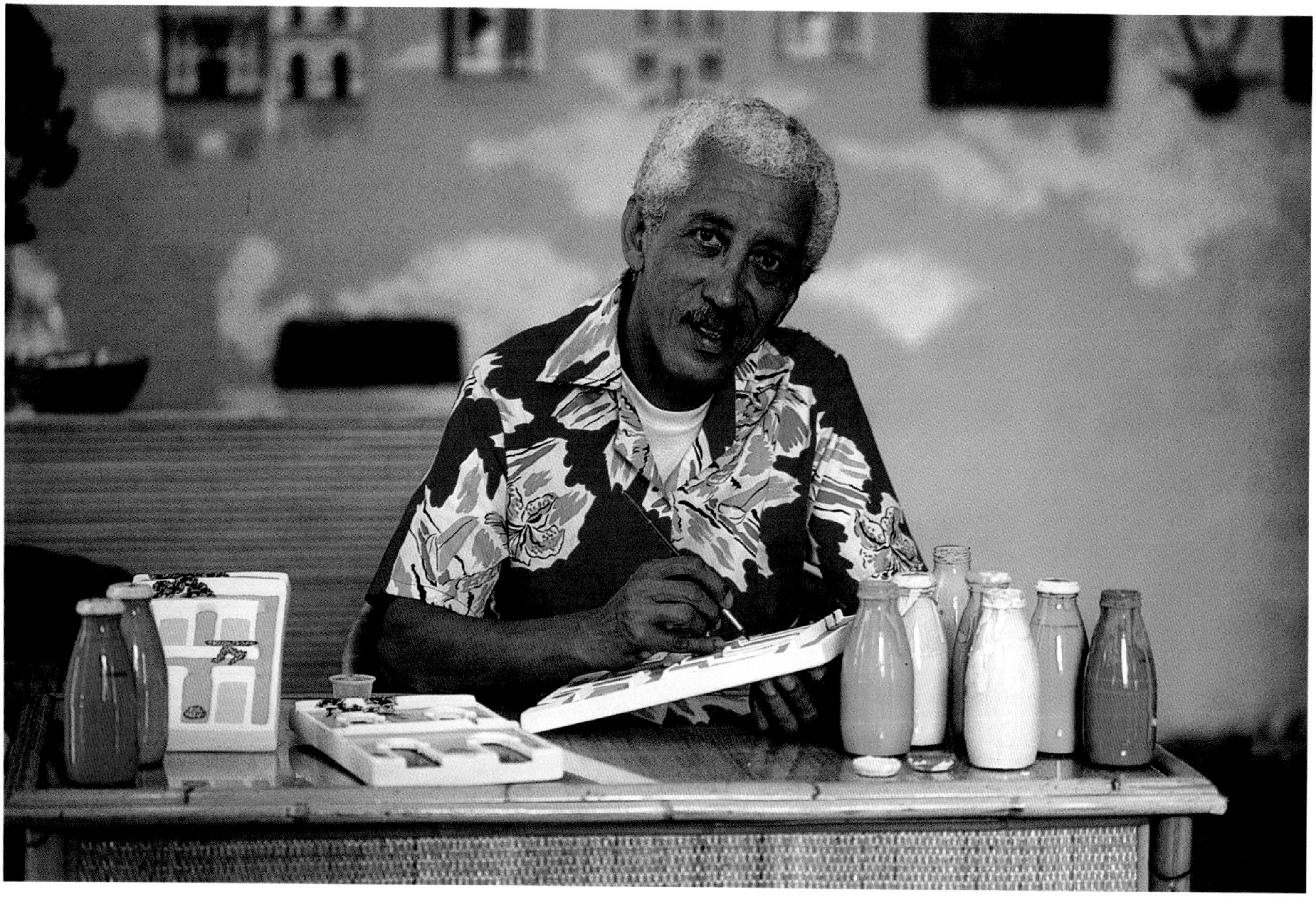

Old San Juan is a haven for artists and artisans of all kinds, and their subject matter is often no further away than the scene outside the window. One of these is Mike Rivera [this page], whose shop on Calle Cristo offers a uniquely realistic view of San Juan's architecture.

He began by selling pieces of painted driftwood to tourists, under a tree across the street from San Juan's Cathedral. "I just about starved in the beginning," he commented. "Then I hit on the idea of painting the houses of Old San Juan. First I did them in wood, then discovered a better way—molding them of a mixture of plaster, cement and clay." The mixture is baked and painted with a white base coat, and then each house facade is individually painted. Each of the models is a faithful reproduction of an existing building in Old San Juan [opposite page].

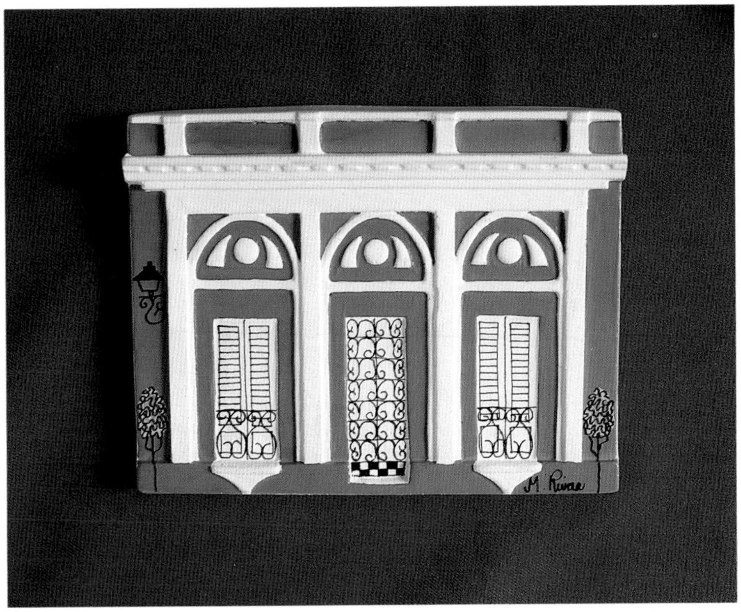

In command of a superb view of San Juan Bay, La Fortaleza was begun in 1533 as the first fortification—hence the name—for the defense of the colony and the harbor entrance. Before the decade was out the growing threat from competing European powers and the vital importance of the bay would lead to the construction of El Morro, overlooking the entrance to the bay, and La Fortaleza would lose its defensive significance. At the same time the colonial governors of the 16th and 17th Centuries began using La Fortaleza—also known as the Santa Catalina Palace—as their place of residence and administrative headquarters, and over the years the building would be adapted and added to with those purposes in mind. (A major reconstruction was undertaken in 1640 after the building was damaged by fire when the Dutch attacked and occupied San Juan in 1625.)

Today La Fortaleza remains the governor's official residence and administrative headquarters, and is the oldest executive mansion in constant use in the Western Hemisphere. Guided tours are available through the public areas of the mansion, including the Hall of Mirrors, used for large formal gatherings [this page, upper], the Informal Dining Room [this page, middle], and the Blue Room, the governor's formal reception room [this page, lower].

Evening brings a special appeal to familiar day-time scenes: the Fuerte de San Gerónimo (also spelled San Jerónimo), which dates from the 16th Century, stands in juxtaposition to the modern-day hotels and condominiums of the Condado area across the Boquerón Inlet [this page]. Beside the superb bay which gave it birth, San Juan glitters under a darkening sky [opposite page].

As the sun falls to the western horizon beyond the Isla de Cabras, many a sanjuanero *strolls the open expanse of park land in front of El Morro to witness the play of light on water . . ..*

Boriquén

For the Taino Indians who called it home, the island was *Boriquén*, "the land of the brave lord." When Columbus and his fellow explorers first saw and visited the island in 1493, it was, according to the reports, covered with trees (although this seems doubtful with respect to the arid southern coastal plain). Although the Tainos were agriculturalists and engaged in some farming, they had had relatively little physical impact on the land, working as they did with no more than stone tools and without animal-drawn plows. Thus the island was largely as nature had evolved her when the Spanish arrived to colonize.

The transformation was hardly immediate: the island's population hardly grew at all during the first decades, and only slowly during its first three centuries. Hindered by a lack of roads into the interior mountains, most farming was limited to the wetter areas of the easily tilled coastal plain. Then in the course of the 1800s the population began a rapid expansion, multiplying more than six times over to nearly a million by the close of the century (a density of approximately 275 people per square mile). Since 1898 the population has tripled again, and with this population explosion, and the rise of tobacco and coffee cultivation, came the invasion of the mountains, and the felling of the virgin forests for farmland and fuel. (In 1950, the nadir, a bare ten percent of the original forest cover remained; today, following the exodus of the *jíbaro* from the interior mountains toward the island's cities and to the mainland, the amount of the island's surface covered by forest stands at about 25 percent.)

To fly low over Puerto Rico in a small plane is to see the impact: scarcely a mountain ridge, especially in the area to the south and southwest of San Juan, without a highway lined with houses, mostly the weekend and summer homes of city dwellers eager to escape the heat, humidity and congestion of the metropolitan area. (For a photographer always in search of unspoiled vistas this is particularly frustrating, for even where there are no houses there are often power lines or radio communications antennas—all part and parcel of "progress" the world over.)

Fortunately, a few pristine areas do remain: undoubtedly and deservedly the most famous is the El Yunque rain forest (or in the parlance of the U.S. Forest Service, the Caribbean National Forest, Luquillo Division), which is the only large area of the island preserved more or less as the first Spanish explorers saw it. And through the efforts of a private, non-profit organization, the Conservation Trust of Puerto Rico (or as it is known in Spanish, the Fideicomiso de Conservación de Puerto Rico), a number of exquisite wilderness areas, such as the Cabezas de San Juan headlands in the northeastern corner of the island, are being purchased and protected from the development which is rapidly spreading throughout the island.

The first Spanish colonists searched the island for gold, and found a bit on the slopes of the mountain they called El Yunque *(the anvil) for the shape of its peak; the waterfall near the mine is still known as La Mina Falls [See page 8 in the introduction].*

Today's explorers of the El Yunque Rain Forest [this page], where over 200 inches of rain fall each year, are after treasures of a different sort, such as this waterfall on Quebrada de Juan Diego [opposite page], and a fantastic variety of animal and plant life.

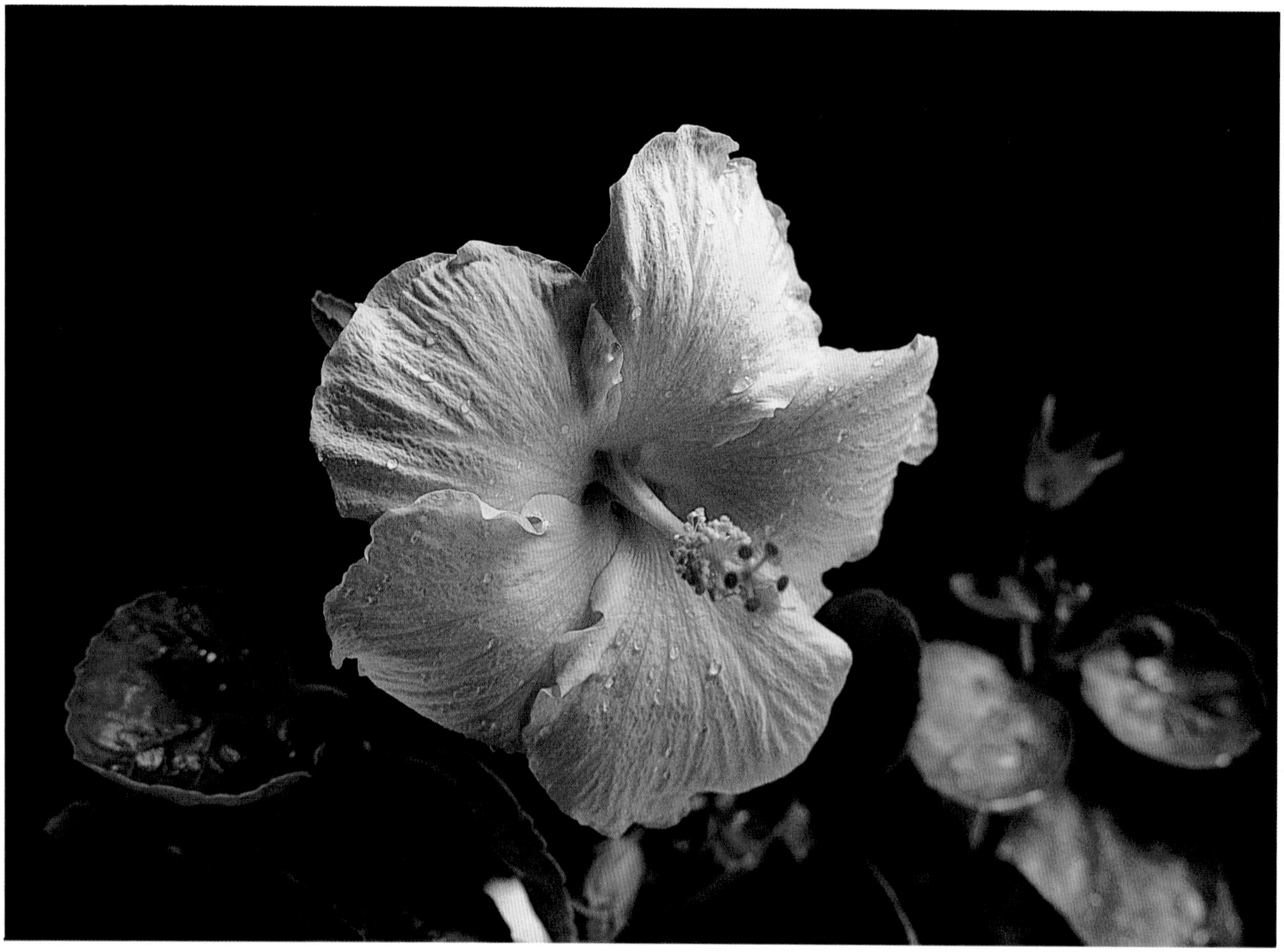

Sentimental symbol and mascot of the island, the singing tree frog, known popularly as the coquí *(ko-KEE), is familiar nighttime accompaniment in almost all parts of the island [opposite page]. Only the males emit the mating call from which the tiny creatures take their name; contrary to popular myth, the frogs can and do exist on other islands of the Caribbean, but nowhere else do they figure so prominently in the popular culture.*

Just as widespread throughout the island is the hibiscus, whose varieties, thanks to hybrids, number in the hundreds worldwide [this page].

As is the case with most islands, Puerto Rico's varieties of animal life were never extensive, and the great changes to habitat imposed by a high population density have further threatened the indigenous species. While the Puerto Rican short-eared owl, known locally as the múcaro sabanero *or the* múcaro real *[*Asio flammeus*; opposite page] continues to thrive desite those changes, the Puerto Rican parrot [*Amazona vittata*; this page] has been fighting a narrow battle with extinction for the past few decades, and now is found only in the remote regions of the El Yunque rain forest. The parrot had nearly vanished by 1971, when fewer than 20 birds were known to exist, but a captive breeding program run by the U.S. Fish & Wildlife Service has been slowly rebuilding the flock.*

The island's considerable range of climatic conditions support a profusion of tropical blossoms, from the prosaic allamanda, a climbing vine [this page], to exotic orchids [opposite page].

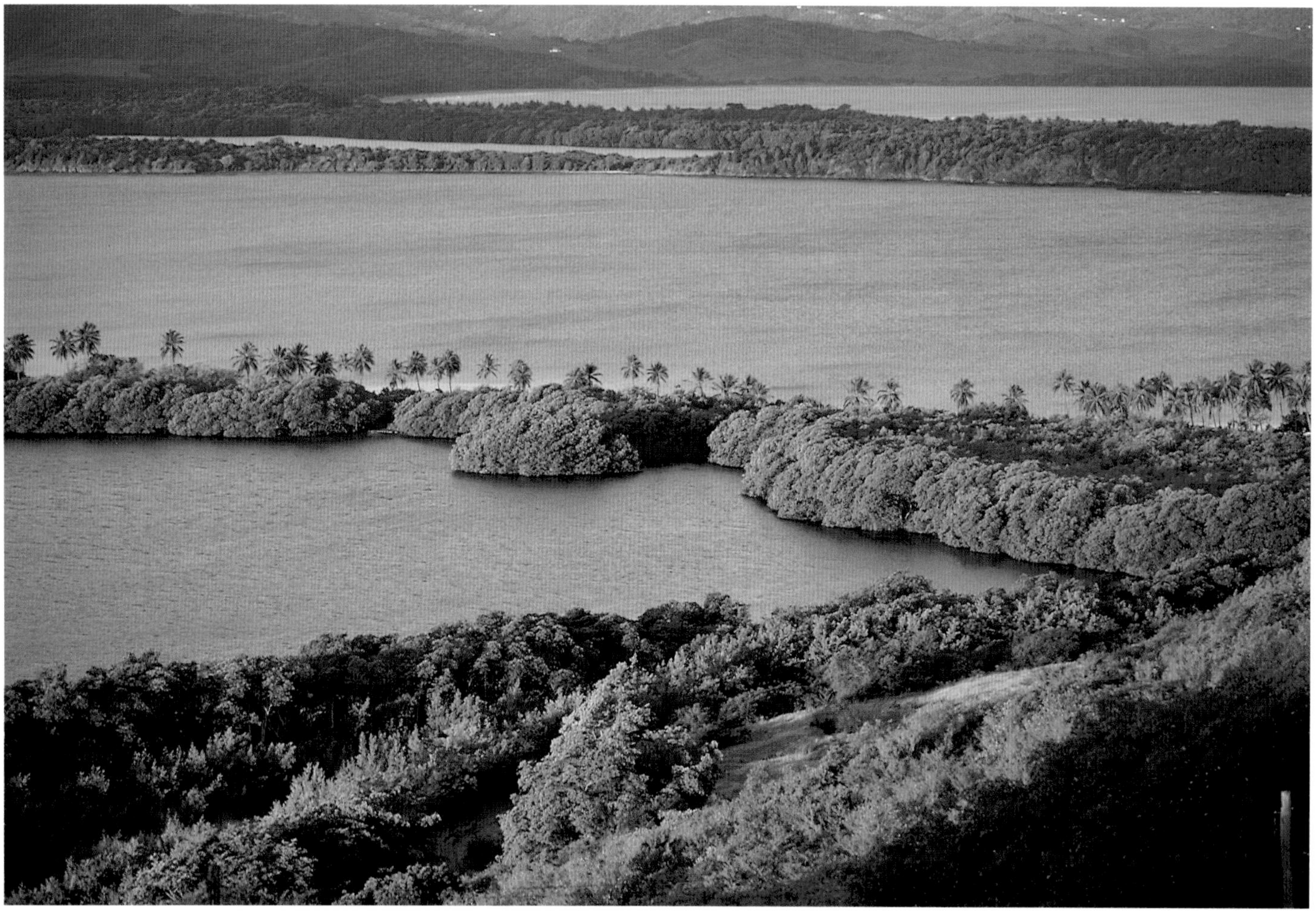

Despite a population density of nearly a thousand people per square mile, pristine areas are still be found in Puerto Rico, including the headlands and lagoons of Cabezas de San Juan [this page] at the northeastern corner of the island (a property of the Conservation Trust of Puerto Rico), and the beaches of Culebra Island, such as this magnificent stretch of sand just east of Flamenco Beach [opposite page].

A Few Boricuas

It is relatively easy to portray a place in photographs; very much harder to portray a people. The reason is no doubt obvious: the former is highly visual; the latter, a complex blend of history, culture, and economics, most of which is invisible. Rather, these elements must be learned through contact and understanding, and here the camera is of little help.

It is further true that in a book of this size and format it is impossible to do justice to the diversity of people who make up Puerto Rico. Thus, I have included this brief section on a few Puerto Ricans (or *Boricuas*, as they frequently call themselves) with some trepidation, for it goes without saying that it unavoidably excludes a great many people deserving of mention.

It should first be said that the people depicted here represent a highly personal selection, based on a distillation of my contact with the island over the past decade, and the same considerations which apply to the process of selecting photographs for this book in general (as I explain below in "Borinquen Querida") apply with particular emphasis to the selection of the few individuals who are shown on the following pages.

There are also some practical considerations governing the selection of people for this section. My first book, *Images of Puerto Rico*, portrays a number of distinguished Puerto Ricans (for example, Lorenzo Homar and Francisco Rodón in the arts; Dr. Ricardo Alegría, in cultural preservation; and a number of the island's outstanding artisans), and I have preferred to give space here to others rather than to repeat those subjects, outstanding though they are. Also, in a few instances, people I would like to have included were simply not available during my time on the island.

It is not suggested for a moment that the people presented herein constitute a full cross-section of the Puerto Rican people. But hopefully each adds a bit to the "story," that is Puerto Rico, and so helps the reader better understand the rich diversity of this island.

A living legend in the eyes of her countrymen, Sister Isolina Ferré of the Missionary Servants of the Most Blessed Trinity has dedicated her life to working with the disadvantaged. After a career working in the neighborhoods of New York she returned to her native Ponce in 1969 and founded the Centro de Orientación *in Playa de Ponce, one of that city's poorest barrios.*

Today the center is famous throughout the island for its aggressive approach to countering the potential for youth delinquency, offering both academic and vocational courses to over two thousand members of the community.

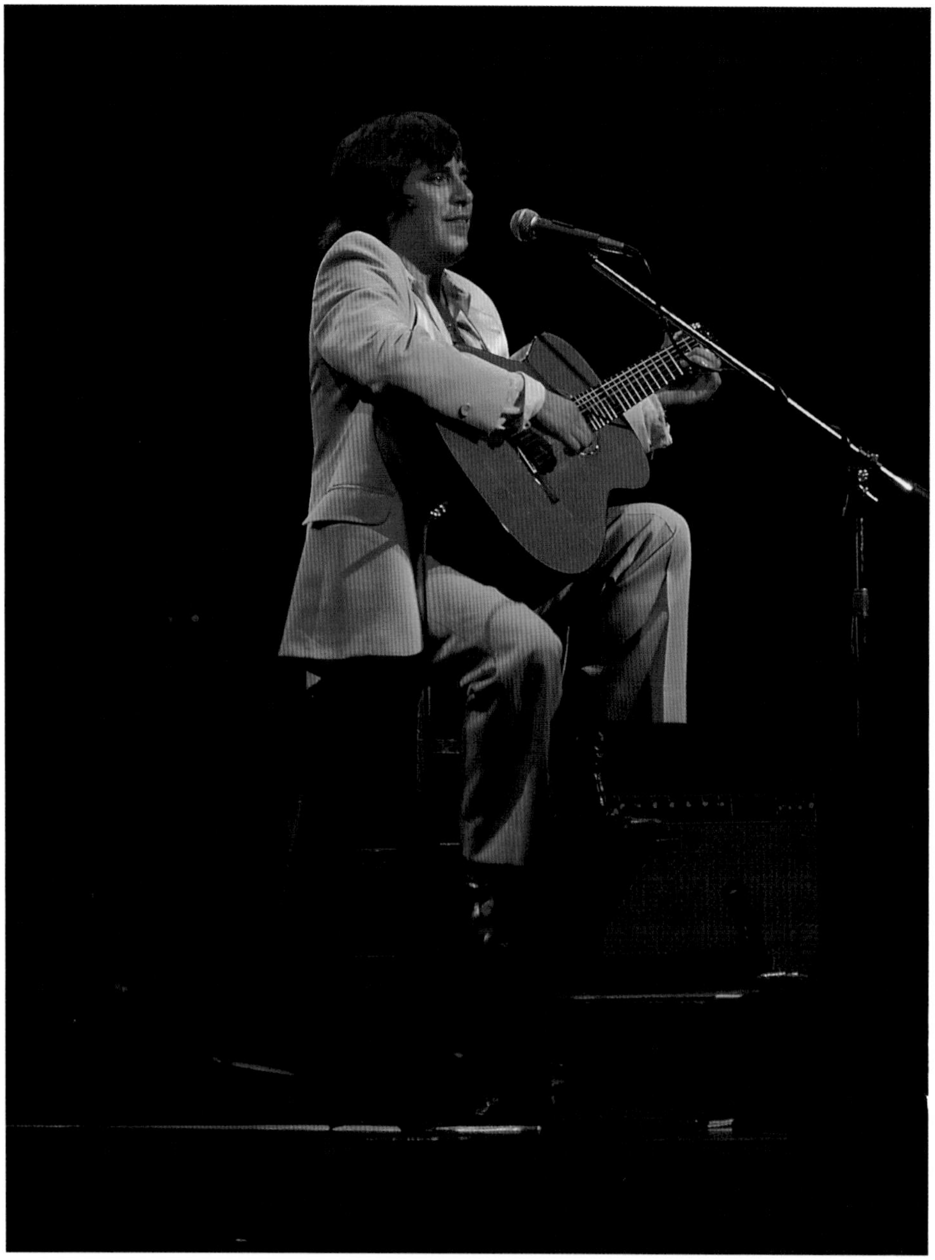

The dance troupe Areyto [opposite page] is the oldest and best known of the island's folkloric groups. The distinctive voice and virtuoso guitar skills of José Feliciano, a native of Lares, have made him an international star in two languages for three decades [this page].

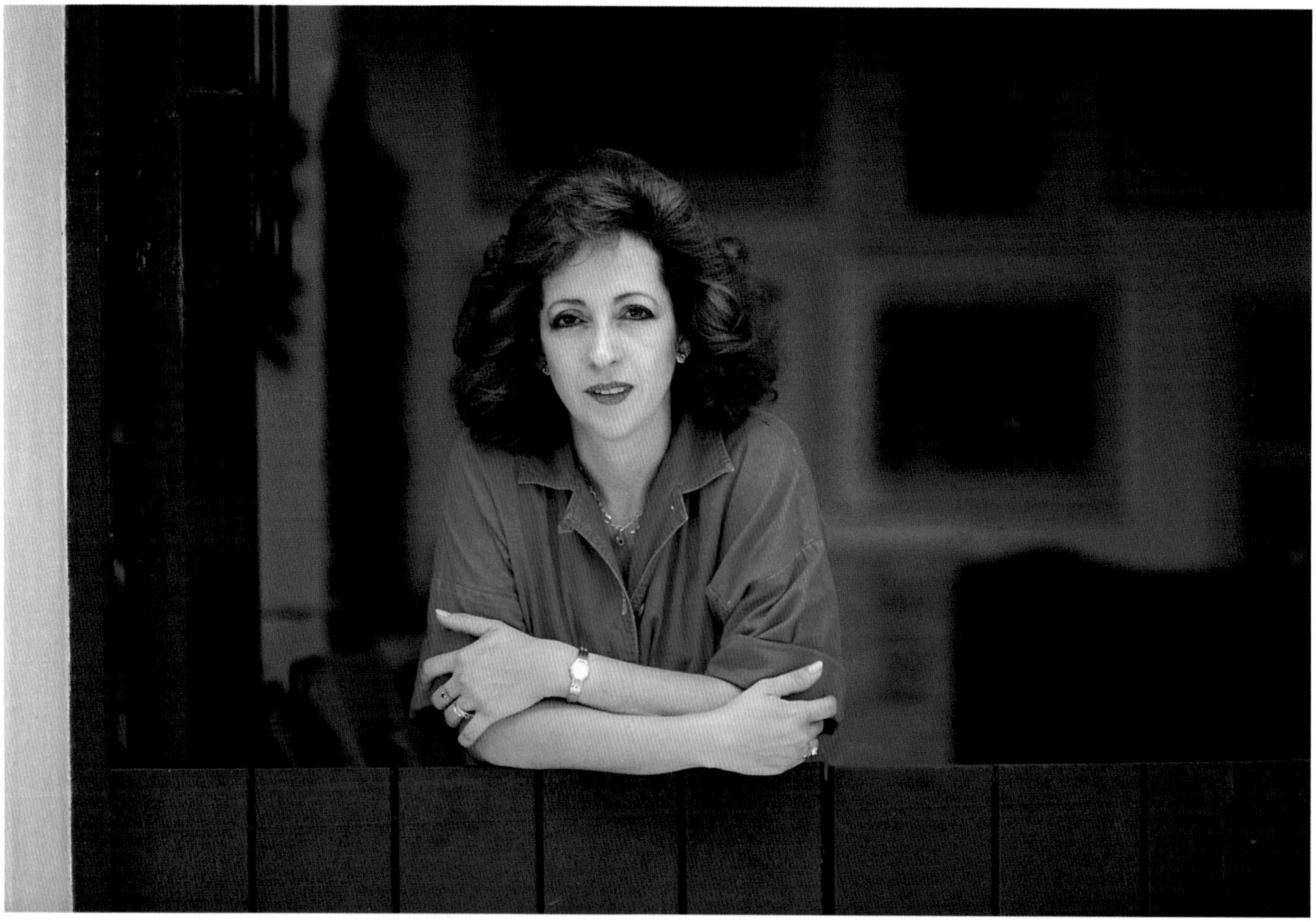

Of all Puerto Rico's artistic formats, none is more highly developed—nor more appealing to me personally—than the silk-screened posters which are used all over the island to publicize cultural events and to honor outstanding individuals in all fields. On this and the following two spreads are the portraits and posters of three of the outstanding graphic artists working today:

Lyzette Rosado is an artist working in Old San Juan whose softer style is already making her a standout name among the younger poster-makers of the island. Woman artists remain a small minority, because, as she puts it, "This is still a very machista *society; many people think a woman should stay in the home, cooking and cleaning."*

ADMINISTRACION DE FOMENTO ECONOMICO
LAS ARTESANIAS SON ALMA Y ESPIRITU DE NUESTRO PUEBLO
MIGUEL CARABALLO PADRE E HIJO
7MA SERIE PUERTO RICO
Ponce

En las montañas de Adjuntas
está un gigante dormido
de agrestes frondas vestido
y su barba al sol despunta
Fiestas Patronales de Adjuntas
P.R.
21-30 de julio de 1989
Administración Municipal

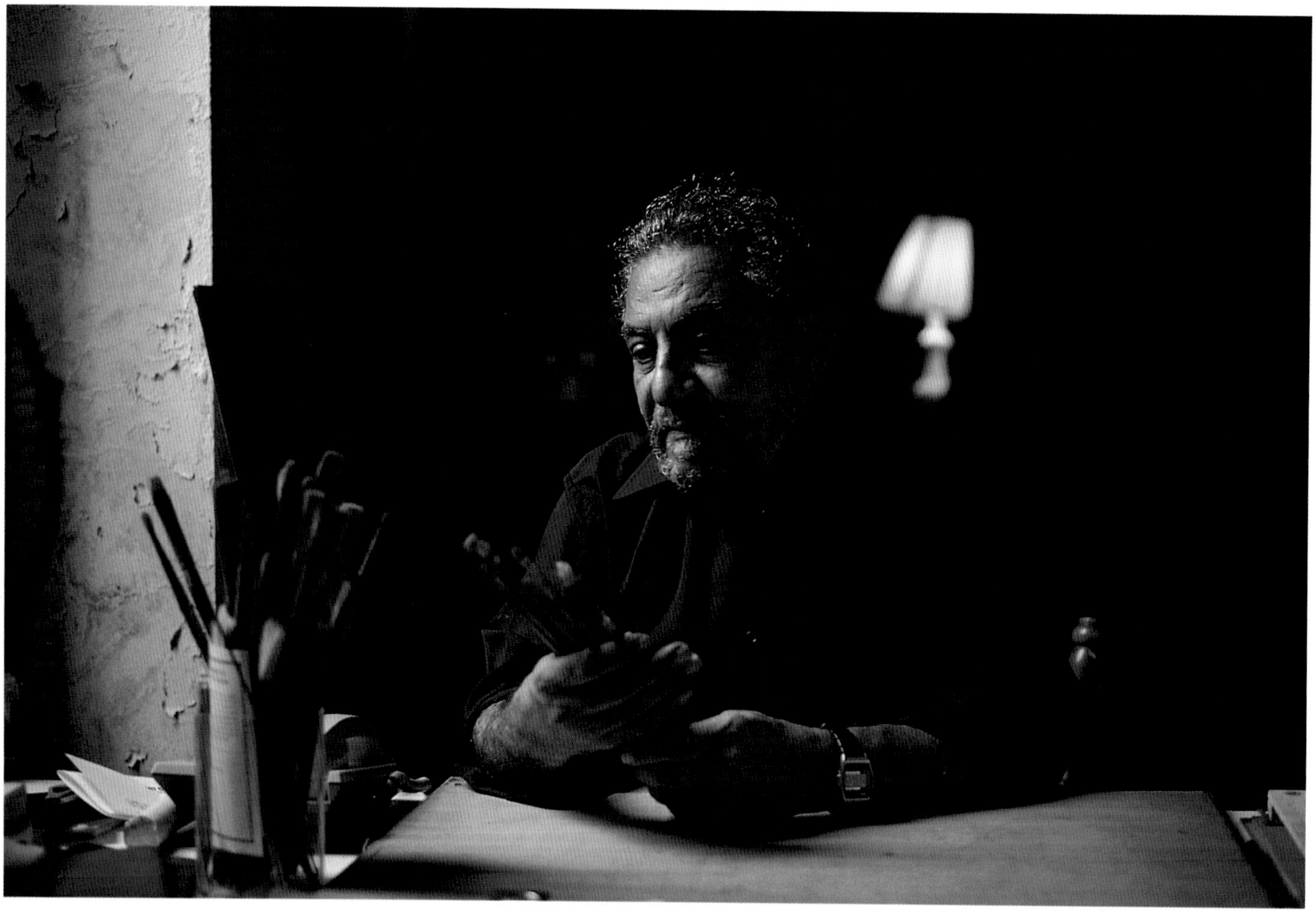

The two acknowledged pioneers in the medium of silk-screening are Lorenzo Homar (whom I featured in my earlier book, Images of Puerto Rico*) and Rafael Tufiño, seen here. Born in Brooklyn of Puerto Rican parents, he divided his childhood between the island and the mainland. After service in the U.S. Army, "Tefo" as he is known to his friends, returned to Puerto Rico, where he was one of the founders of the Puerto Rican Art Center.*

I was curious about the creative process by which he is able to dream up the often incredibly inventive designs which characterize many of the posters. "I'll be damned if I know!" he said with a laugh. "I start making little sketches, and eventually one of them just evolves into the finished work!"

(The poster on the right depicts Luis Muñoz Rivera, who is often referred to as the "George Washington of Puerto Rico" for his early pioneering role in the autonomist movement.)

CENTRO DE RECEPCIONES DE GOBIERNO SAN JUAN DE
PUERTO RICO DEL 12 AL 23 DE JULIO DE 1985
TORNEO DE AJEDREZ LUIS MUÑOZ RIVERA
FIDE
GENS UNA SUMUS

José Alicea, a native of Ponce and once a student of Lorenzo Homar's, is today himself a professor at the School of Plastic Arts (where this photograph was taken). In a career spanning four decades he has had scores of one-man shows, and his work is in the collections of both the Metropolitan Museum and the Museum of Modern Art in New York City. In 1987 his poster design was selected by the Commission for the 5th Centennial of the Discovery of America and Puerto Rico.

OBRA
GRAFICA
DE JOSE R
ALICEA
Exposición retrospectiva
en ocasión del 442 do aniversario de
LA UNIVERSIDAD AUTONOMA
DE SANTO DOMINGO
en la
GALERIA
DE ARTE MODERNO
del 24 de OCTUBRE al 7 de NOVIEMBRE

PUERTO RICO
Capital artesanal del Caribe
1985
ADMINISTRACION DE ASUNTOS FEDERALES DE PUERTO RICO EN WASHINGTON
1984

ADM. FOMENTO * ECONOMICO
CECILIA CATALA
YAUCO
LAS ARTESANIAS SON ALMA
Y EMBRUJO DE NUESTRA TIERRA
10ma SERIE PUERTO RICO 1987

del 17 al 19 de julio de 1987
26 TA FERIA NACIONAL
DE ARTESANIAS
DE
BARRANQUITAS
INSTITUTO DE CULTURA PUERTORRIQUEÑA · CENTRO CULTURAL
LUIS MUÑOZ RIVERA · MUNICIPIO DE BARRANQUITAS

Inspired by its rich Carnival tradition, Ponce is home to a number of master mask-makers, including Leonardo Pagán. Like many artisans, he worked at other jobs for most of his life in order to make ends meet. It is only now, in retirement, that he is able to devote full time to creating his masks, which are built up with layers of moistened paper on concrete molds, then painted.

Perhaps the most unusual craft is that of octogenarian Emilio Rosado, who has been carving wooden roosters—some of which sell for hundreds of dollars—at his home workshop in Utuado for over five decades. In 1990 Mr. Rosado joined a handful of Puerto Rican artisans who have been honored by the National Endowment for the Arts.

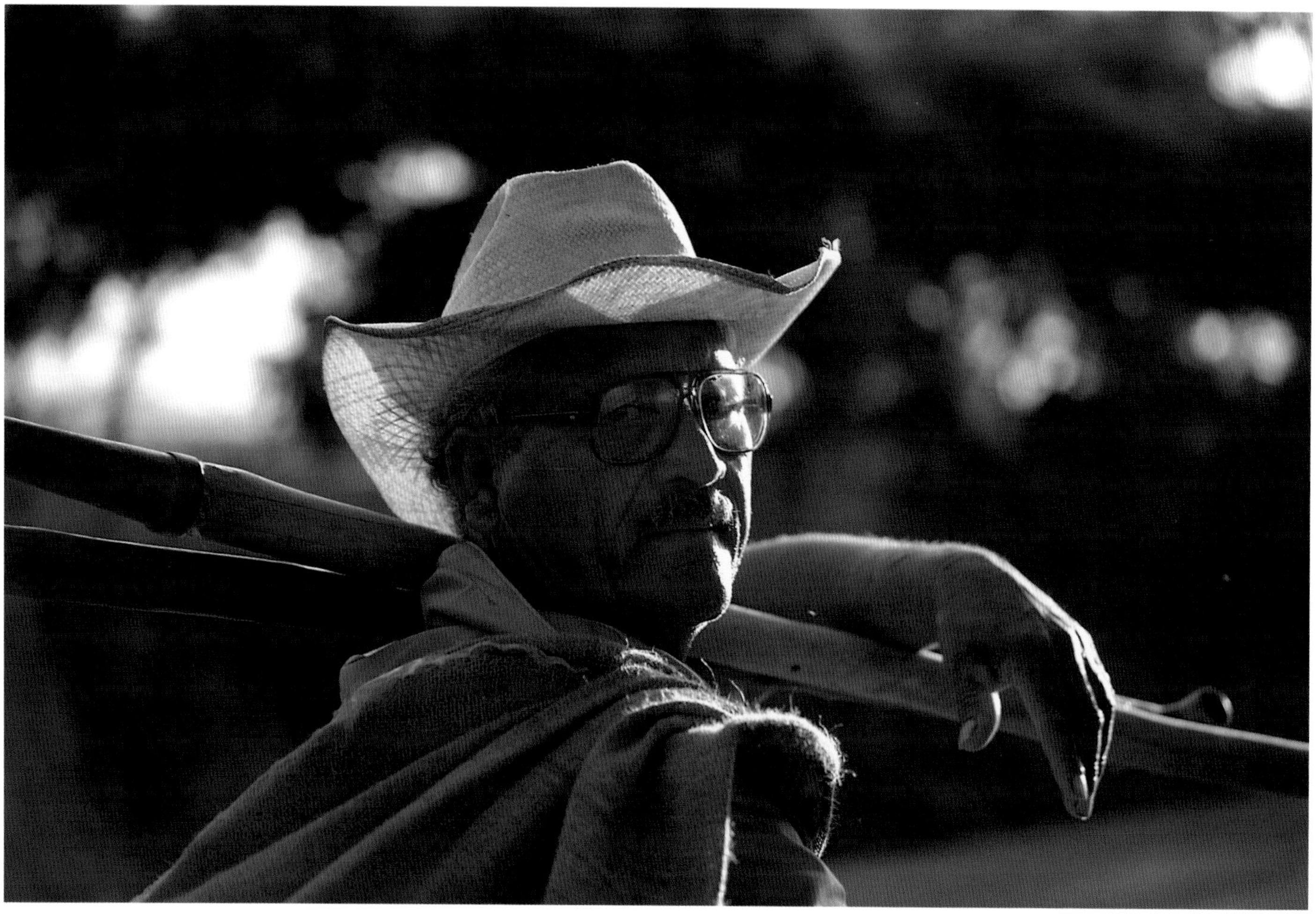

Symbol of Puerto Rico's rural past, the jíbaro *is ennobled in a monument next to the Ponce-San Juan freeway high in the Cordillera Central. The statue's inscription reads:*

The jíbaro is the man of our land, the cultivator of our soil, the genesis of our people, and the authentic expression of Puerto Rico

The jíbaro has always been the symbol of our collective identity and the synthesis of the virtues of the people of Puerto Rico

To the Puerto Rican jíbaro homage from a grateful people

As Puerto Ricans migrate steadily toward the mainland and the island's cities, the man who tills his own soil in the mountains of the island, like Juan Morales of Adjuntas [this page], is a rapidly vanishing breed.

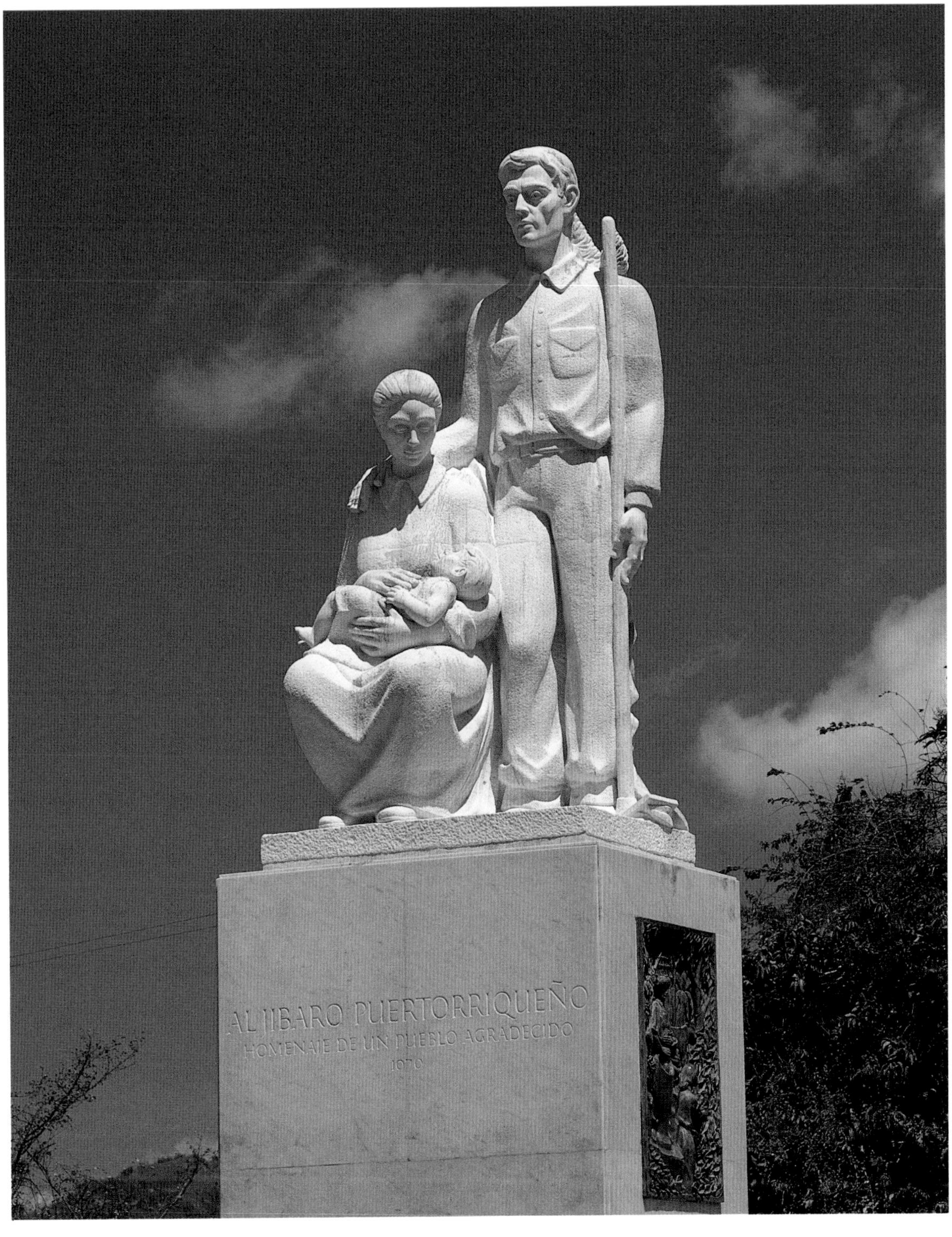
AL JIBARO PUERTORRIQUEÑO
HOMENAJE DE UN PUEBLO AGRADECIDO

La Isla

In standard Spanish, the title of this chapter means "the island"; but in Puerto Rican parlance, it refers to that part of the island outside of the San Juan metropolitan area. In the course of this century, *la isla* has been transformed, undergoing the same rural-urban migration which has taken place in the mainland USA and throughout much of the world: in 1900 over eighty percent of the Puerto Rican population was rural. As the end of the 20th Century approaches, nearly eighty percent of the island's inhabitants live in its cities and towns.

The growth of the San Juan metropolitan area has been alluded to in a previous chapter. But in the same period the cities and towns outside the capital area have also seen explosive population growth, in many cases doubling or tripling in the past few decades.

No factor has been more important in this transformation than the automobile and the network of paved roads which reach into every corner and interior valley of the island. (The automobile, while liberating to the individual Puerto Rican, has not always been kind to Puerto Rico itself: the traffic congestion in the San Juan area is well known, but many of the smaller cities, whose streets were laid out before every household had a car or two, also suffer from traffic jams.) Where forty years ago the *bohíos* of the *jíbaros* were dotted on their tiny plots of land across the landscape, now people are more likely to live in an urban area and work in one of the hundreds of factories set up throughout the island under the "Operation Bootstrap" program.

For all that, the soul of the average Puerto Rican lies in the *campo*, the rural setting which gave birth to the *jíbaro*, the man of the soil who, despite the radical changes in the decades since the end of the Second World War, remains the symbolic precursor of today's Puerto Rico. Thus it is perhaps only just that the car and the highway now enable *Boricuas* to escape their predominantly urban environment, and every weekend the roads are crowded with people heading to beachside or mountain retreats, or perhaps going to see family or friends in Lares, Adjuntas, Yabucoa, or Aguadilla, or wherever "home" may still be, out on *la isla*, where the heart is.

Sugar cane "in arrow" glistens in the setting sun. For decades King Sugar dominated the island's economy as well as its landscape. Buffetted by foreign competition and rising labor costs, decline set in during the 1950s, and today the industry has nearly disappeared from the Puerto Rican scene.

Symbol of tropical paradise, a row of coconut palms near Rincón is silhouetted against the Mona Passage.

The cascade of the Sierra de Cayey into the sea at the southeast corner of the island [this page] creates one of the most dramatic landscapes in all Puerto Rico. Cayo de Luis Peña, an island gem, floats in pristine seas off Culebra Island [opposite page].

An aerial view of swampland near Arroyo on the southern coast [this page]. The northern littoral west of San Juan is characterized by the hummocks and sinkholes of a rare karst formation, known in Puerto Rico as mogotes *[opposite page]. Underground rivers have carved spectacular caves from the underlying limestone in the region near Arecibo.*

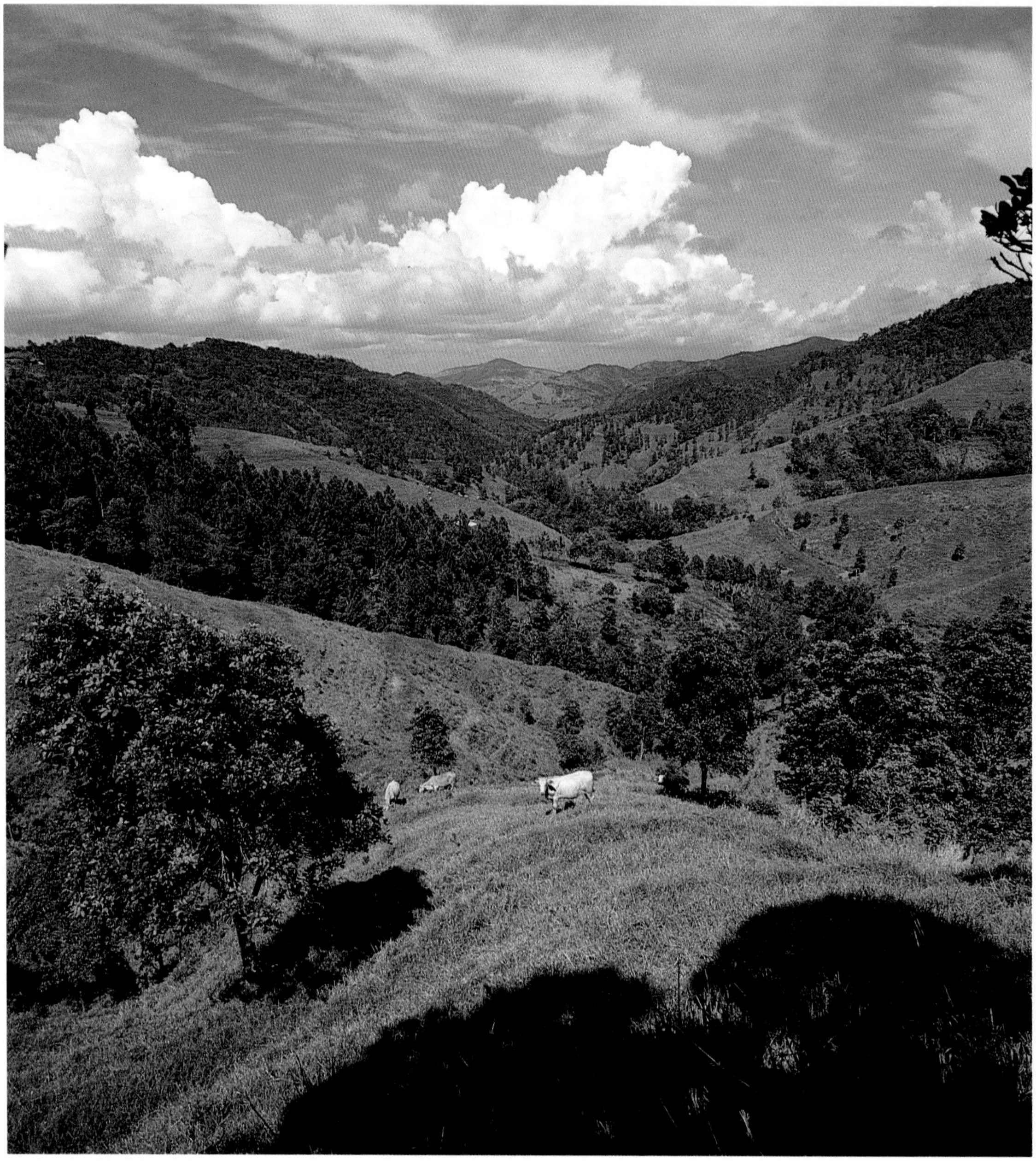

The steady exodus of the jíbaro *to the island's cities and to the mainland and the decline of coffee, tobacco, and subsistence farming in the mountain areas have seen much cultivated land turned to pasture, for the raising of beef and dairy cattle [this page]. The* jíbaro *exodus has hardly left the mountains without houses, however: coastal city dwellers, seeking relief from tropical heat, have covered the mountain ridges with weekend and summer homes, especially near the San Juan metropolitan area [opposite].*

Founded in 1512, San Germán is the second oldest city in Puerto Rico [this page, one of the city's two plazas]. The city's nickname, "La Ciudad de las Lomas," reflects its pride in being beautifully situated on hills in the southwestern corner of the island.

Mayagüez, dating from 1763, is the "capital" of the western region, and prides itself on its modernity as well as on its ties to the past. The statue of Cristóbal Colón in the city's Plaza Colón [opposite page] commemorates the great discoverer's landing a few miles up the coast in 1493 [opposite page].

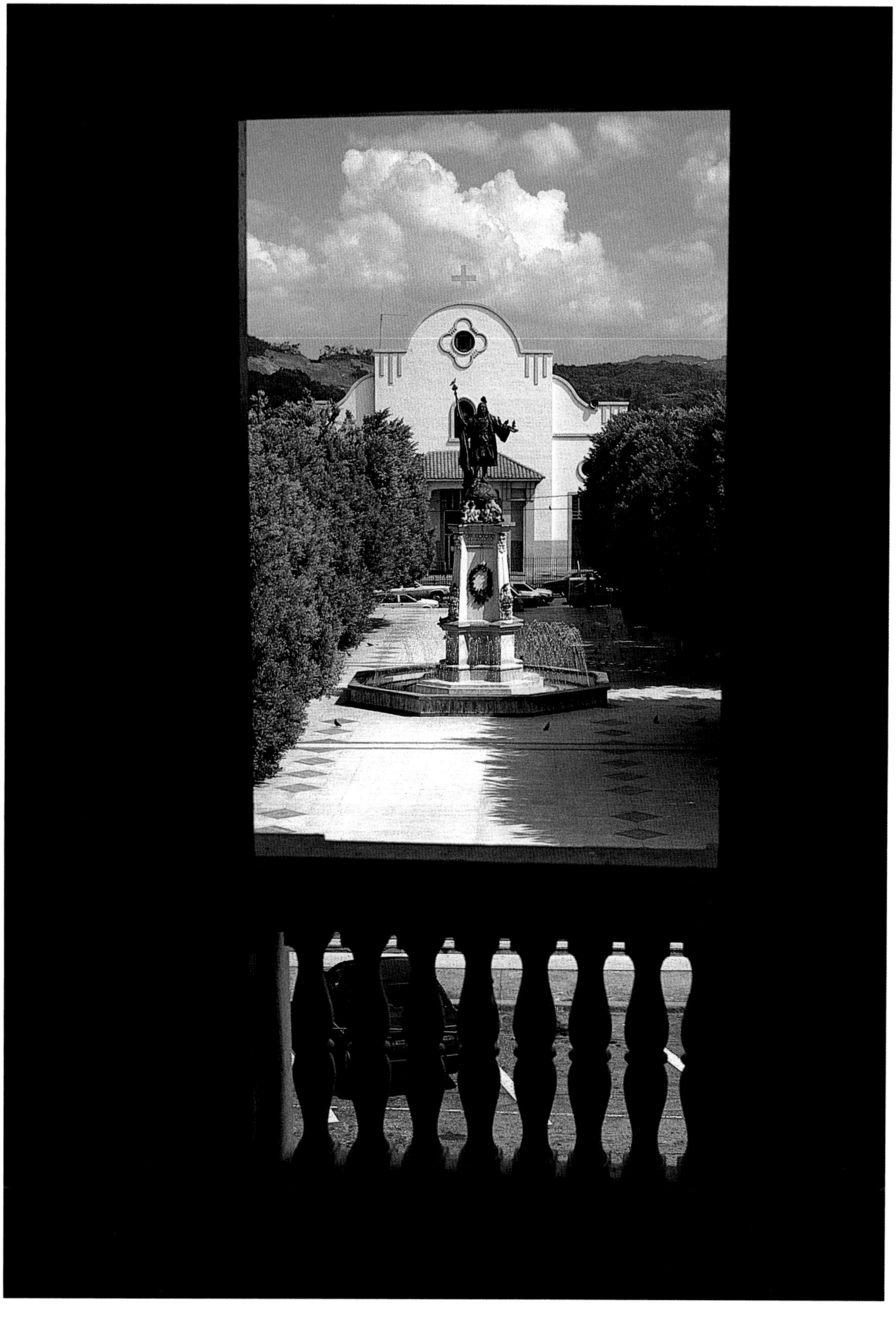

Portfolio: Ponce

La Ciudad Señorial ("the Seignorial City") they call it, and no people on the island are more justified than the people of Ponce, the *ponceños*, for the pride they show in their city. Although it has in recent years been surpassed in population terms by Bayamón, Ponce remains Puerto Rico's traditional "second city," and, like many second cities the world over, unsurpassed in the way it has been able to manage to preserve the traditions of the country's culture and architecture, without ignoring the demands of the modern era. (As is the case with many dates in Puerto Rico, the date of the founding of the city is difficult to establish with certainty, perhaps because "founding" may mean different things. The year 1692 is usually given as the official date, although various authorities cite 1752, 1762, and 1778.)

The heart of Ponce's tradition lies in its central plaza, consisting of the side-by-side Plaza Muñoz Rivera on the north and Plaza Degetau on the south (although I much prefer the historic and lyrical name for the plaza, Plaza de las Delicias, "the Plaza of Delights") with its historic cathedral and firehouse, and sculpted, white-trunked Indian laurels. One can walk in blocks in all directions from the plaza and see and sense the atmosphere of a bygone era, much of it restored under a project sponsored by the city entitled "Ponce en Marcha" (Ponce on the March).

And yet directly facing the plaza are two icons of the late 20th century, and proof that the city does not mindlessly stand in the way of change: a Burger King and a McDonald's, both of which have been so tastefully designed that the buildings add to, rather than detract from, the architectural harmony of the setting. (I wish I could say the same for the record store on the corner of the plaza which, unaccountably, is allowed to blast its outdoor loudspeakers at full volume.)

Nonetheless, a few minutes' drive from the city center reveals that the city has grown explosively in the past two decades: high rises, expressways, and modern housing tracts where a few years ago there were sugar cane fields. The genius of the *ponceños* has been to keep the juggernaut called "progress" in its place, and "Ponce always Ponce."

Ponce's historic La Perla Theater, recently restored under the "Ponce en Marcha" Project.

Plaza Degetau and Plaza Muñoz Rivera together form Ponce's central plaza [these pages], graced by fountains and statues and shaded by sculpted Indian laurels. Surrounding the plaza are some of the most handsome buildings on the island, and its centerpiece is the city's Nuestra Señora de Guadalupe Cathedral, successor to the church founded in the late 17th Century.

BANCO DE PONCE

Ponce's famed Parque de Bombas [opposite page], set in the central plaza behind the cathedral, dates from 1882, the year it was built as an exhibition hall for a church festival; the following year it became a fire house when the city's fire brigade was formed. The red and black of the fire station reflect the city's traditional colors. Calle Isabel [this page] is the showcase for some of Ponce's finest traditional architecture.

PARQUE DE BOMBAS
1883

Some of the architecture which befits Ponce's traditional name, "La Ciudad Señorial" (the Seignorial City)

*In the mountains above Ponce the Conservation Trust of Puerto Rico (*Fideicomiso de Conservación de Puerto Rico*) has restored and operates Hacienda Buena Vista, the finest "living museum" on the island. Originally the property of the Vives family of Ponce, the plantation began life in the 1830s as a producer of various fruits, later producing corn, rice and cotton as well.*

In the later 19th Century the Vives converted the property to coffee production, and it is as a coffee plantation that the hacienda is seen today. Guided tours offer demonstrations (in season) of all stages of coffee processing, as well as a tour of the main house [these pages], whose period furniture and decorations reflect turn-of-the-century plantation life.

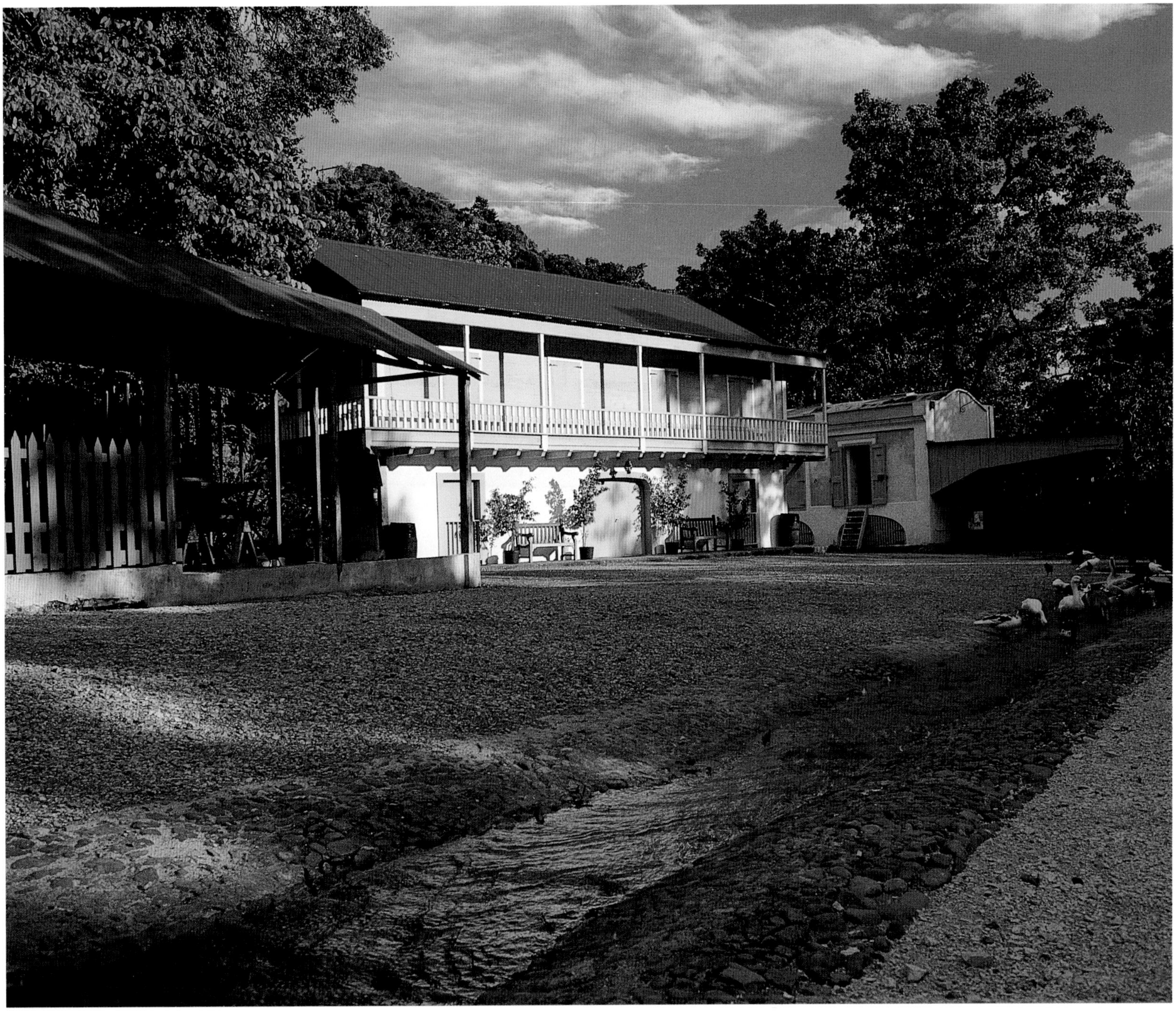

Tropical Playground

A tropical playground, an island in the sun. That is how much of the world thinks of Puerto Rico, as it does its sister islands of the Caribbean. Thus it is more than a little ironic that the attributes which have made Puerto Rico (and the rest of the Caribbean), known to the world during the last forty years are qualities which have been with the islands since time immemorial. And yet it is only since the end of the Second World War that the island's climate, natural features and setting have come to be recognized as priceless assets by both the world at large as well as by Puerto Ricans themselves. The results have been the creation of tourism as a key industry for the Puerto Rican economy and a significant change in the lifestyle of many Puerto Ricans themselves.

The underpinnings of these economic and social changes are twofold and both are technological: the development of the airliner, and the spread of air conditioning. The first made possible the movement of large masses of people over great distances very quickly, the second made their stay bearable once they arrived at their destination in the tropics. Coupled with these technological advances were two further post-war essentials: the rise of a large, affluent middle class in North America (and to a lesser extent in Europe), and a newfound fondness for going out in the blazing sun to get a tan.

As large numbers of American and Canadian tourists began descending on Puerto Rico with regularity, Puerto Ricans themselves began discovering the treasure of sun, sand and sea they had surrounding them. Gradually the idea of a tanned skin became acceptable, then fashionable, eventually displacing the traditional bias which held that the lighter one's skin, the better.

I recall reading some years ago in an old issue of *National Geographic Magazine* that most of Puerto Rico's beaches "out on the island" were deserted during the winter months, because "Puerto Ricans don't go to the beach in winter." No longer: today the island's beaches are a playground all year around, and it is Puerto Ricans themselves who most value their island in the sun.

The setting sun brings magic to Punta Agujereada at the northwest corner of the island.

Mild tropical ocean temperatures and beautiful beaches on the west coast near Cabo Rojo, often deserted during the week, lure beach lovers throughout the year.

The west coast near Rincón offers some of the finest conditions for surfing, while the north coast is a favorite of windsurfers. [Surfing photograph: Craig Fineman]

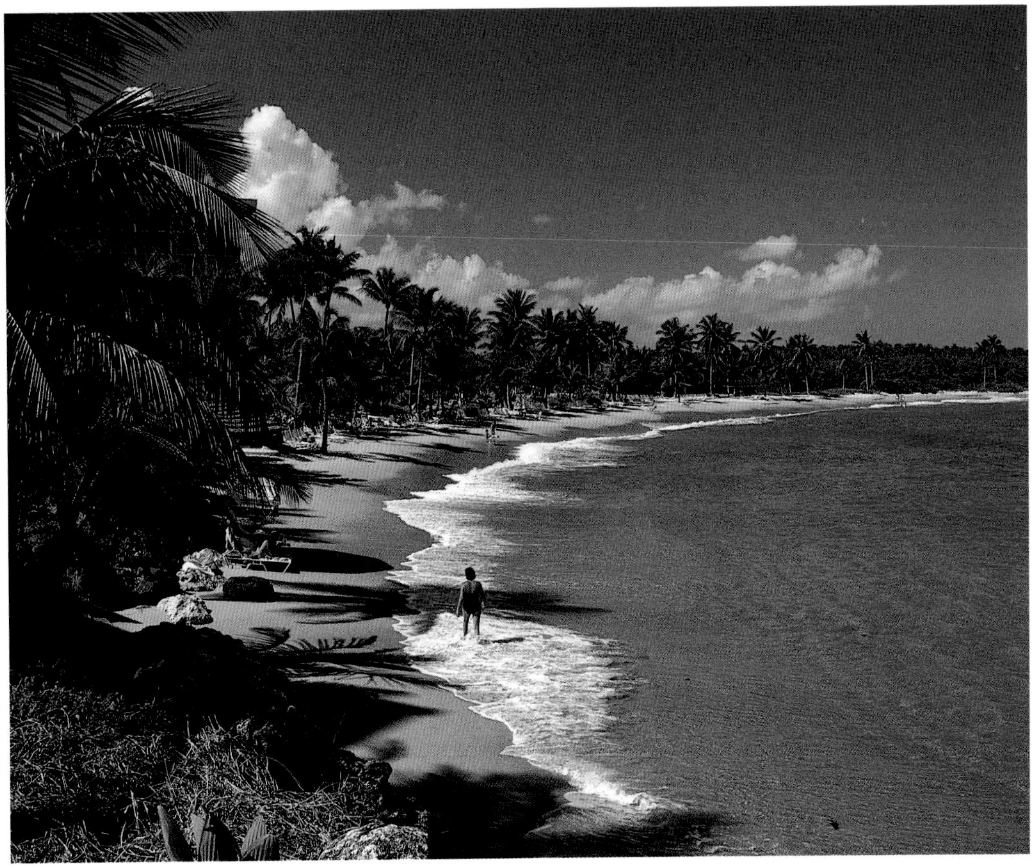

Although many of Puerto Rico's deluxe hotels are to be found in the greater San Juan area, some of the largest and most luxurious resorts are located out on the island. First developed during the 1950s, the Dorado-Cerromar complex [above, the beach at Cerromar] is widely considered the grande dame of these resort hotels.

In 1993 the spectacular El Conquistador Resort and Country Club opened on a magnificent site near Fajardo, in the northeastern corner of the island. Among the hotel's many features are a superb pool area [these pages], and a private "fantasy island" a few hundred yards offshore.

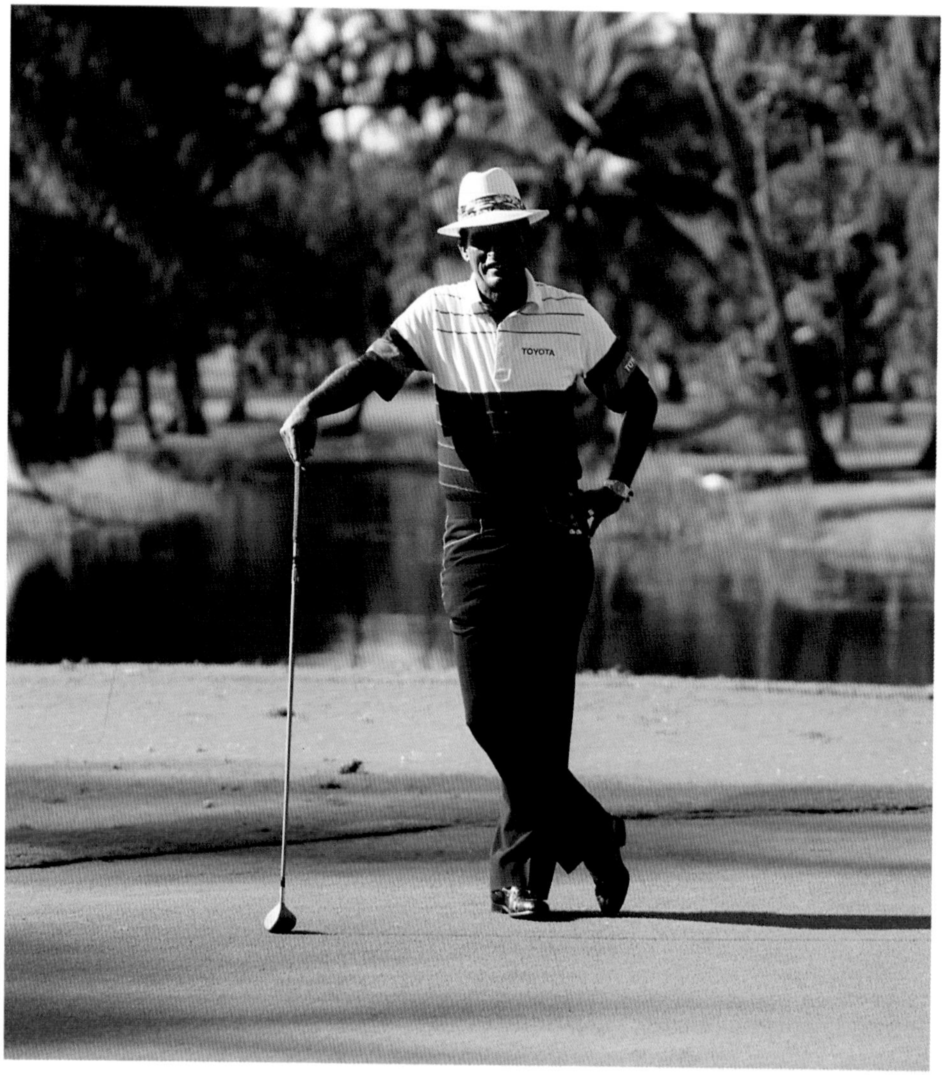

Always at ease on a golf course, Chi Chi Rodriguez [this page] is Puerto Rico's golfing ambassador to the world, as well known for his irrepressible personality as for his sporting exploits. Less well known is his extensive charity work: during his visit to the island when I made this photograph, he was meeting with the governor to set up a foundation for island youth.

Among the most famous of the island's golf courses, and its most beautiful, is the course at the Dorado Beach resort, built by Laurence Rockefeller in the late 1950s [opposite page].

In the past two decades San Juan's excellent harbor and airline connections, together with the island's central location, has made it an important port for a dozen cruise ships plying the Caribbean.

Borinquen Querida

One of the most complex and difficult aspects of putting a book like this together is deciding what is to be included and what must be left out. I refer here not only to the actual editing process, but to the original coverage itself; that is, what to photograph and research. To a great extent this is for me an intuitive process, arrived at almost through an unthinking process of osmosis over the period of months I typically spend in a place doing the photography and research for one of my books.

People in the profession often express surprise at the uncommon length of time, normally between six months and a year, I spend on location photography when I undertake a book project. Perhaps it is my Peace Corps experience that compels me to feel that it requires at least that much time to come to even an elementary understanding of the place I am covering, and thus to grasp its essence and attempt to capture it on film as well as in words. And yet, despite this investment of time, it should go without saying that any book of this nature is by necessity only a limited view of a place, its people, and its culture. Hopefully to some extent the limitations to understanding inherent in being an outsider are offset by the different perspective which can lead to insights sometimes overlooked by the native.

A further complexity involves the organization of the photographs that are finally chosen: some fall logically into categories, and these become sections or chapters. Others are not so easily classified, and yet they communicate something which I find captivating and essential to the "story" of a place; hence this section, and with it, the opportunity for a final personal note.

Mi Borinquen querida. My beloved Borinquen. I first came to Puerto Rico over two decades ago, very much by chance, and without a thought that the island would become a part of my life for many years into the future. By turns intriguing, captivating, frustrating, mystifying, sometimes infuriating . . . but in the end, enchanting and thoroughly unforgettable.

Many times over the past decade or so I have thought I had at last come to understand Puerto Rico, only to then discover a new level of complexity. Now I know better than to imagine that I will ever fully fathom this island. I console myself with the thought that, *si dios quiere*—God willing—I will nonetheless be able to continue trying for many years to come.

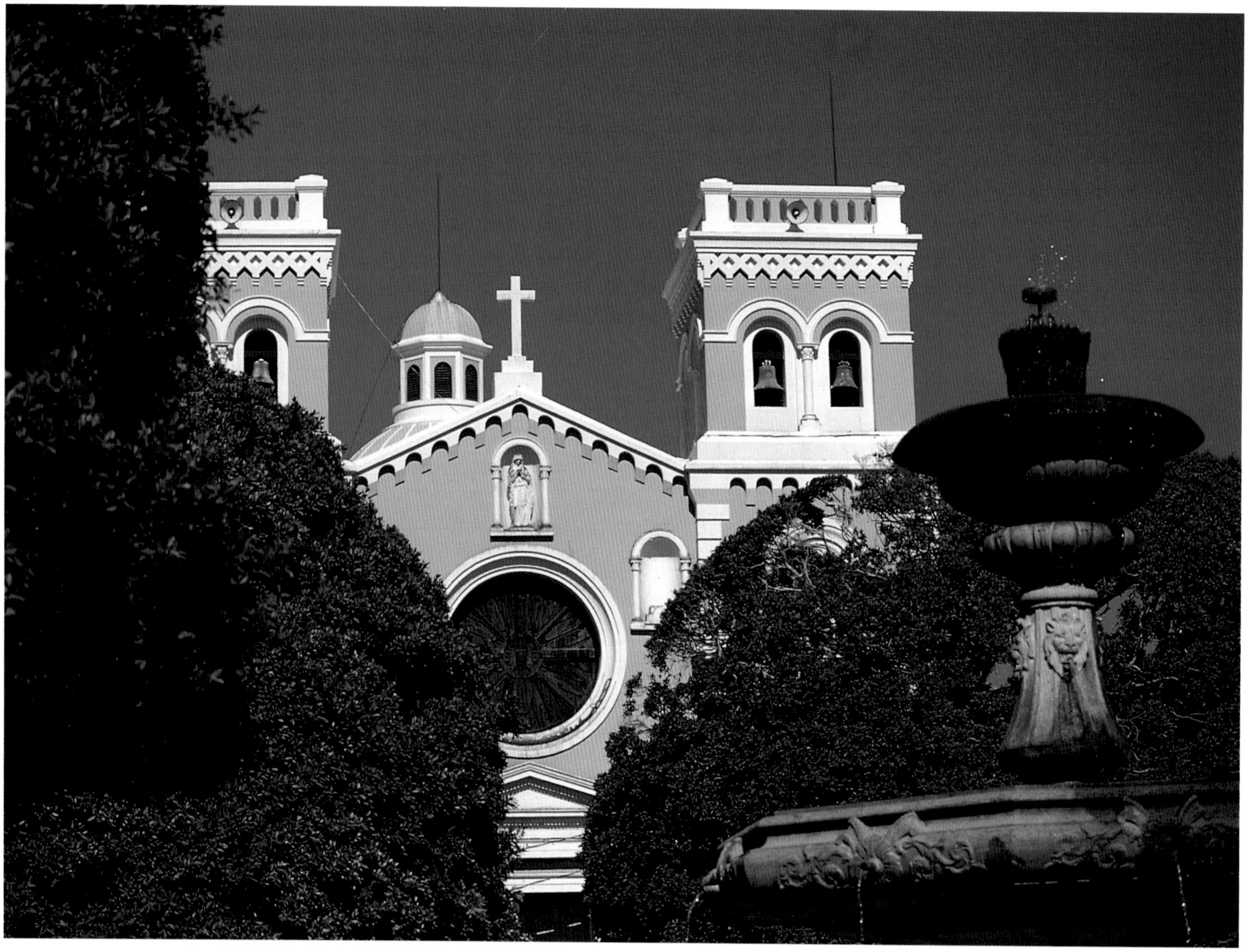

Two outstanding examples of Puerto Rico's striking variety of architecture: the San Antonio de Padua Church in Guayama [this page], and the Capitol in San Juan, seat of the island's legislature [opposite page].

TRANSITO

Handiwork of two of the island's masters of traditional crafts, both of whom are featured in the chapter entitled "A Few Boricuas": a rooster carved by Emilio Rosado of Utuado [this page]; and masks created by Leonardo Pagán of Ponce. Originally used in Ponce's Carnival celebration, the many-horned masks are now widely purchased for use as decorations [opposite page].

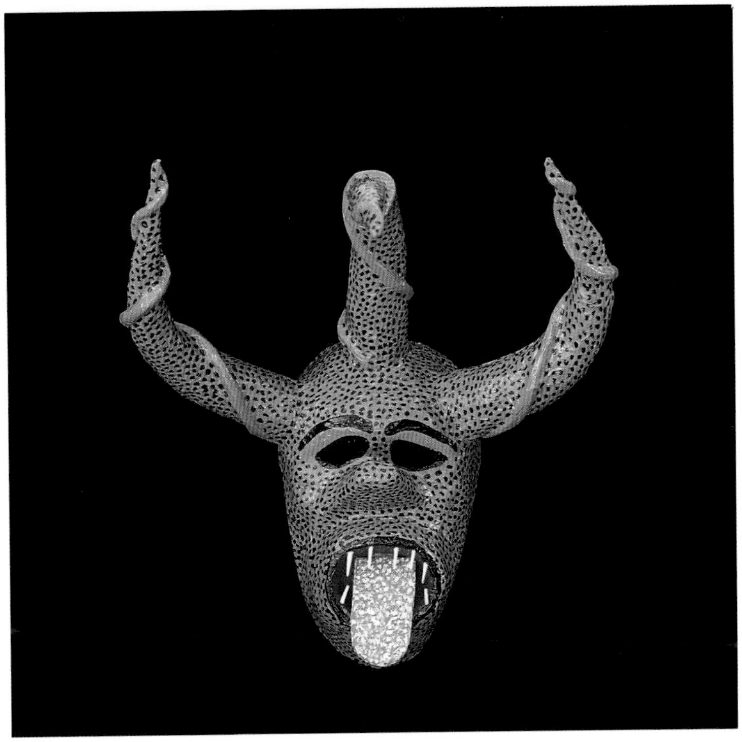

The lights of the Esteves Bridge come aglow as evening falls over San Juan [this page]. Signature of the Old City, the blue-tinted adoquines *which pave many of its narrow streets first reached Puerto Rico as ballast in the holds of sailing ships [opposite page].*

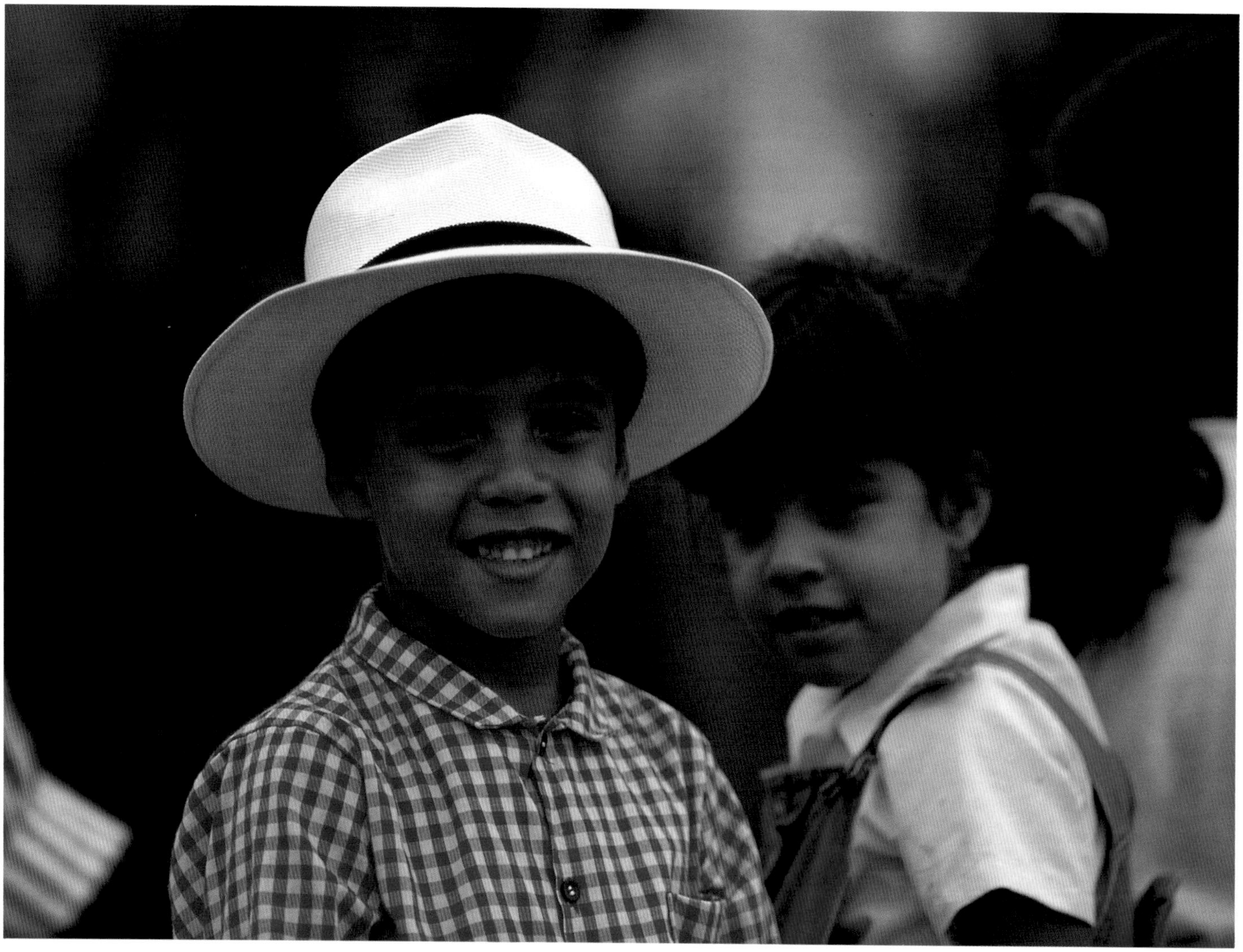

Brother and sister José and Dariam Ramos gaze into the camera at a paso fino *horse show in Trujillo Alto [this page]. Hopefuls for future Olympic Games, young gymnasts mug for the camera at their training center in Carolina, a suburb of San Juan. Puerto Rico sends its own delegation to the Olympic Games under its own flag, many of whom train at a superb new training center near Salinas on the southern plain [opposite page].*

AMERICAN
VORTEX

An inviting feature of Puerto Rican life and its cultural landscape is the fact that tropical weather allows open-air living the year round: one aspect of that lifestyle is a tremendous variety of roadside stands, offering a great variety of food as well as souvenir items.

Winston

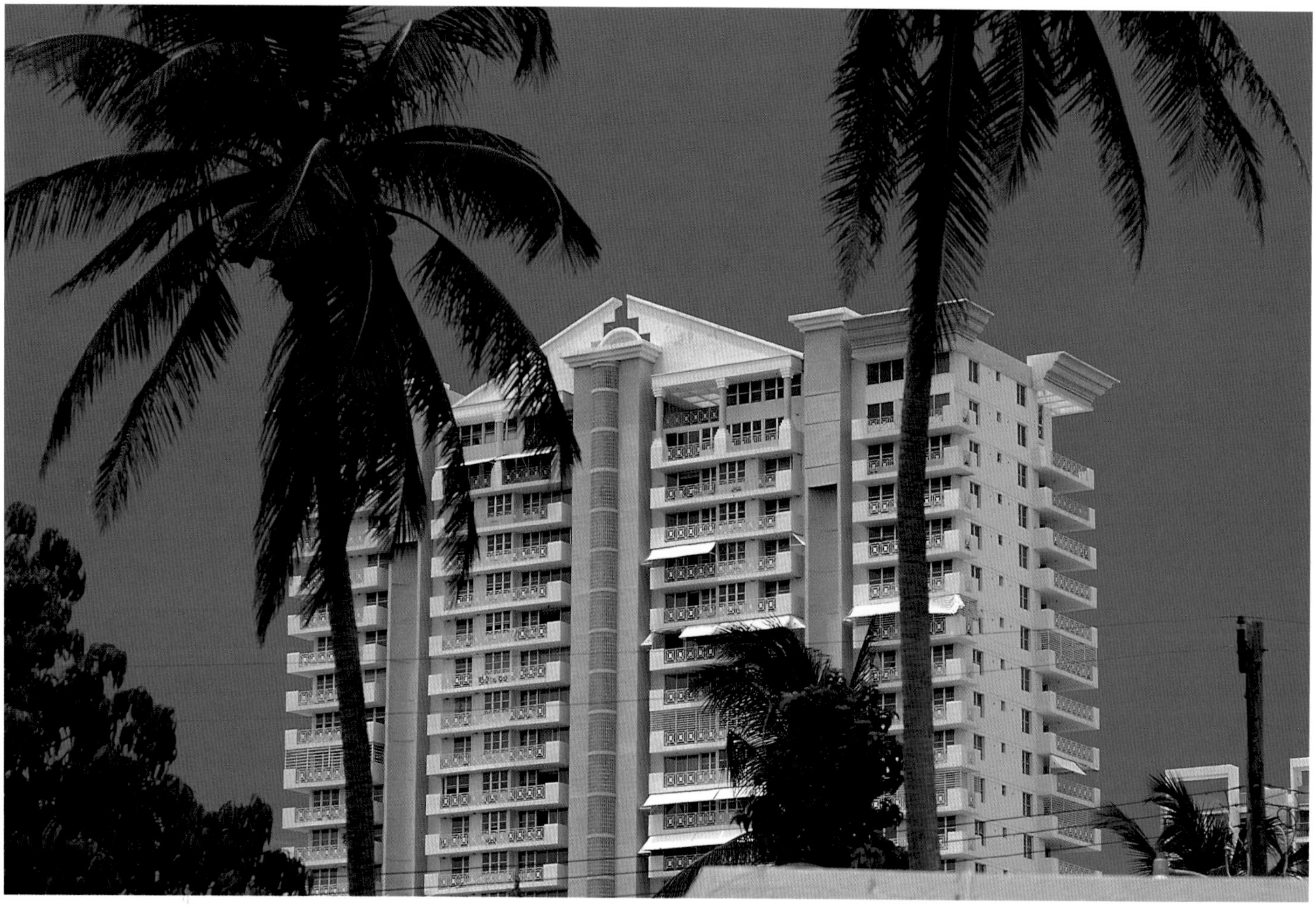

The Church of Santa Ana, in Old San Juan, dates from the 16th Century, and was restored to its present form in 1848 [opposite page]; in contrast, the roofline of a modern high-rise condominium, dating from the late 20th Century [this page].

A sampling of the endless variations of colors and forms lending enchantment to the architecture of Old San Juan.

Indian laurels, or "fig trees" (derived from the Latin word ficus*), with their often fantastic sculpture of aerial roots, decorate many of the island's parks [opposite page]. One of the most beautiful blossoms of the island's flowering trees:* Reina de las flores, *"Queen of Flowers" [this page].*

A morning mist hangs over Lago Dos Bocas, near Utuado [this page]. As is the case with all of Puerto Rico's mountain lakes, Dos Bocas is man-made, created to feed the island's water supply system and for flood control.

At day's end, a lone fisherman appears to have a spectacular sunset over the Ensenada de Boca Vieja, near Cataño, all to himself [opposite page].

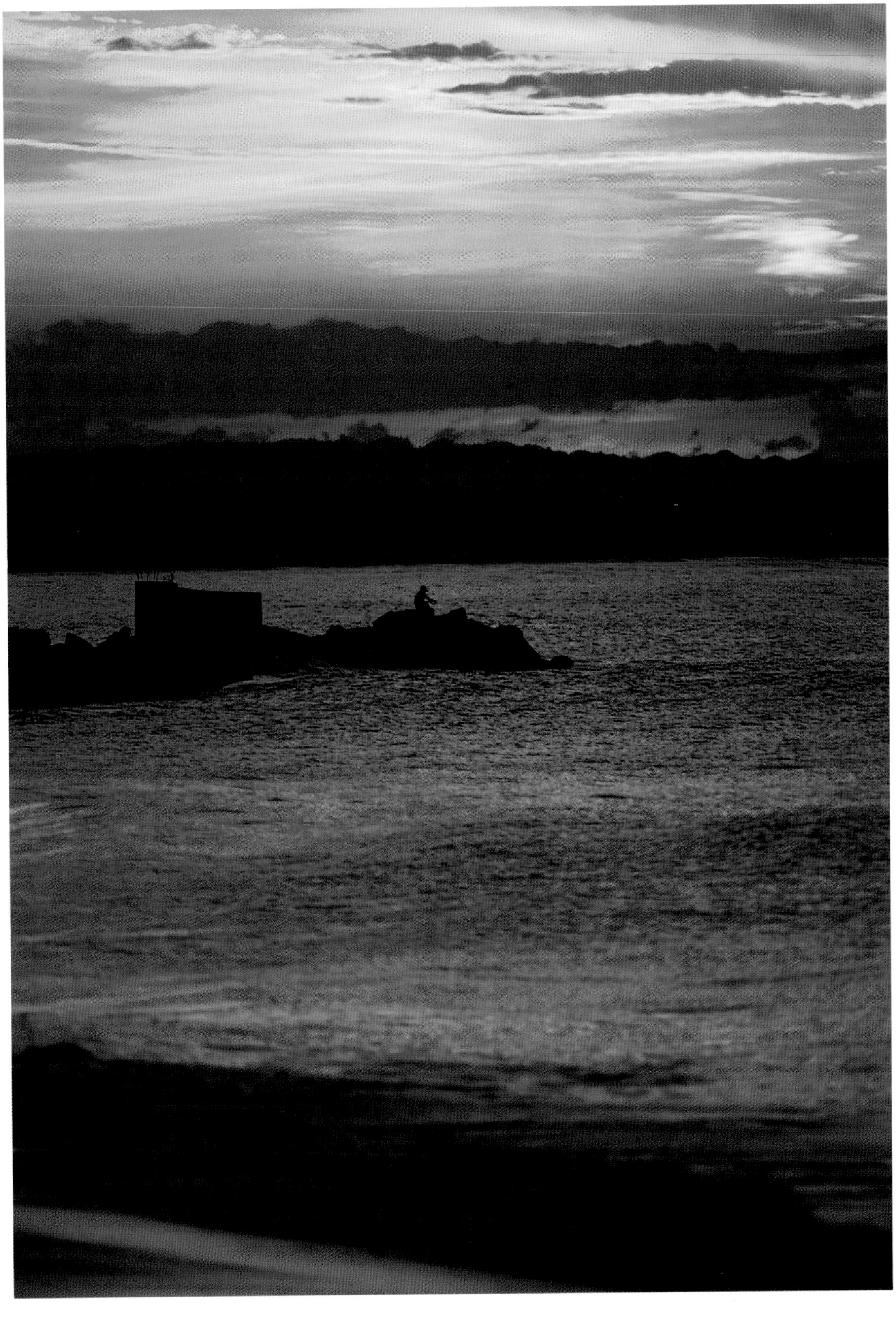

Corporate Sponsors

Production of a book of this nature inevitably means the assistance of countless individuals and organizations, both public and private. Among the most valued supporters of this project have been the following corporate sponsors, without whose participation this book would never have come into being. It should perhaps be pointed out that, while each of these sponsors has been generous with financial support, none has either sought or been accorded prior review of the content of this book. The opinions expressed are therefore solely those of the author, and he alone is responsible for any errors or omissions which may have escaped notice.

AT&T of Puerto Rico, Inc.
Abbott Laboratories
Able Sales Company, Inc.
Anaquest Caribe, Inc.
The Bared Company of Puerto Rico, Inc.
Barros & Carrión, Inc.
ConAgra - Puerto Rico
Condado Plaza Hotel & Casino
Cortelco Puerto Rico, Inc.
De la Cruz & Associates
El Dorado Technical Services, Inc.
El San Juan Hotel & Casino
Empresas Pagán
Ernst & Young
Ethicon
General Accident Insurance Company Puerto Rico Limited
Glenn International Inc.
Kelly Temporary Services
Kodak Caribbean Ltd.
Motorambar, Inc.
Nestlé Puerto Rico, Inc.
Pfizer Pharmaceuticals, Inc.
Phillips Puerto Rico Core Inc.
Price Waterhouse - San Juan Office
The Procter & Gamble Commercial Company
Productos Electronicos Industriales
Puerto Rico Sun Oil Company
R. J. Reynolds Tobacco Co.
Schering-Plough del Caribe
Schering-Plough Products, Inc. - Manatí Operations
The Shell Company (Puerto Rico) Limited
Superior Packaging Inc.
Western Auto Stores - Puerto Rico

Notes

1. Sources: As will no doubt be apparent to the reader, *Puerto Rico, Borinquen Querida* is essentially a collection of impressions, both verbal and visual, of the island; it is not, nor does it pretend to be, an in-depth analysis of Puerto Rican history, culture, or society. For those seeking more detailed treatment, there are a number of writers, far better positioned than I, who have published numerous such studies. Among them are Arturo Morales Carrión and Kal Wagenheim, just two of the authors on whose works I have relied extensively in preparing this volume; also of great help were Aníbal Sepúlveda Rivera's *San Juan, Historia ilustrada de su desarrollo urbano, 1508-1898*, and *Puerto Rico* by Insight Guides. Other sources utilized were virtually all of the Puerto Rican newspapers during my stays on the island, as well as the standard reference sources. As will be readily apparent from a reading of the text, much of this book is based on personal observation and conversations during the time I spent on the island.

2. Photographic Notes: Most of the photographs for *Puerto Rico, Borinquen Querida* were shot during a period of five months in late 1990. My principal film was Kodachrome 64, although a few shots were made on Kodachrome 25 and Ektachrome 200; I have over the years worked with a number of color films, but for overall quality of both the filmstock and processing, I have yet to find films to surpass Kodak's. (When shooting for reproduction transparency films are generally superior to print films.) I worked with Nikon bodies and lenses, as I have for the past twelve years, because while I feel that there are a number of excellent camera systems, I have found Nikon bodies and lenses unmatched for ruggedness and reliability, an important consideration when shooting on location. Most exposures were made based on the in-camera light meters, although I sometimes use a spot meter and incident meter in difficult lighting situations. I worked with three camera bodies (a Nikon F3 and two Nikon FE's) although I usually carried only two at any one time. Additional bodies facilitate using different films and are essential backups on location. I used ten different Nikkor lenses, varying in focal length from 16mm to 500mm; together with many other photographers, I find the Nikkor 105mm to be superb for portraiture as well as a great deal of general shooting; my 24mm and 180mm lenses also saw a great deal of use.

I am occasionally asked what differentiates an amateur from a professional photographer; there are of course a number of factors, of which equipment is one. But to my mind the essential difference can be summarized as follows: an amateur *takes* pictures, while a professional *makes* pictures. By this I mean that any photograph a professional expects to publish is usually the end result of a fairly involved process which begins with an idea, or concept, and is followed by planning and preparation. The eventual snapping of the shutter is often a fairly small part of the whole process. This means that a professional must have the time and resources to go back repeatedly to redo a shot (especially where nature is involved) until it comes out as he had hoped or envisioned. And of course as a general matter in publishing photographs it never hurts to have a large number of shots from which to select: the photographs appearing in this book, for example, were chosen from over 15,000 of my original transparencies.

Puerto Rico

Location and geography: the smallest and easternmost of the Greater Antilles, Puerto Rico lies between the island of Hispaniola, 75 miles to the west across the Mona Passage, and the Virgin Islands, some 40 miles to the east. The island measures approximately 110 miles east to west, and 35 miles north to south. Total area: 3435 square miles (8897 square kilometers), including its adjacent islands, of which Vieques, Culebra and Mona are the largest. The interior of the island presents a rugged mountainous aspect, which characterizes about three fourths of its area; the dominant range, with elevations above 3,000 feet, is the Cordillera Central, running east to west somewhat to the south of the center of the island. Highest island elevation: 4389 feet (1338 meters) at Cerro de Punta.
Population (1990): 3,522,000 inhabitants (about 1025 persons per square mile). Major municipalities and populations: San Juan (capital): 437,700; Bayamón: 220,300; Ponce: 187,700; Carolina: 177,800; Mayagüez: 100,300; Caguas: 133,000.
Government: since 1952, a commonwealth in voluntary association with the United States; officially, the Commonwealth of Puerto Rico, or Estado Libre Asociado de Puerto Rico ("Free Associated State of Puerto Rico"), in Spanish. Essentially self-governing under the Constitution of Puerto Rico in all internal matters, although federal law governs in many areas (including the currency, post office, customs and immigration). Universal adult suffrage elects a governor and a bicameral legislature; the judiciary completes the tripartite governmental structure. Puerto Ricans are U.S. citizens, with all the incumbent rights and obligations; U.S. citizens resident in Puerto Rico have no vote in federal elections and pay no federal tax on island-generated income.
Economy: based principally on manufacturing (pharmaceuticals, electronics, clothing, textiles, etc.); the trade, finance, insurance, real estate, and tourism sectors follow in economic importance; agriculture, which until 1955 remained the largest sector, now provides a meager two percent of total employment. Per capita personal income (1989): $5650.
Climate: tropical; along the north coast mean temperature varies from 80°F. (27°C.) in summer to 75°F. (24°C.) in winter, with about 60" (1500mm) of rainfall distributed fairly evenly throughout the year, heaviest from May to December. The south coast is drier and somewhat warmer; the interior mountains, considerably cooler. Temperatures are moderated by the nearly constant northeasterly trade winds.
Miscelaneous: Language: Spanish; English is widely spoken. Religion: predominantly Roman Catholic, significant minority of Protestant adherents; complete freedom of religion and separation of church and state.

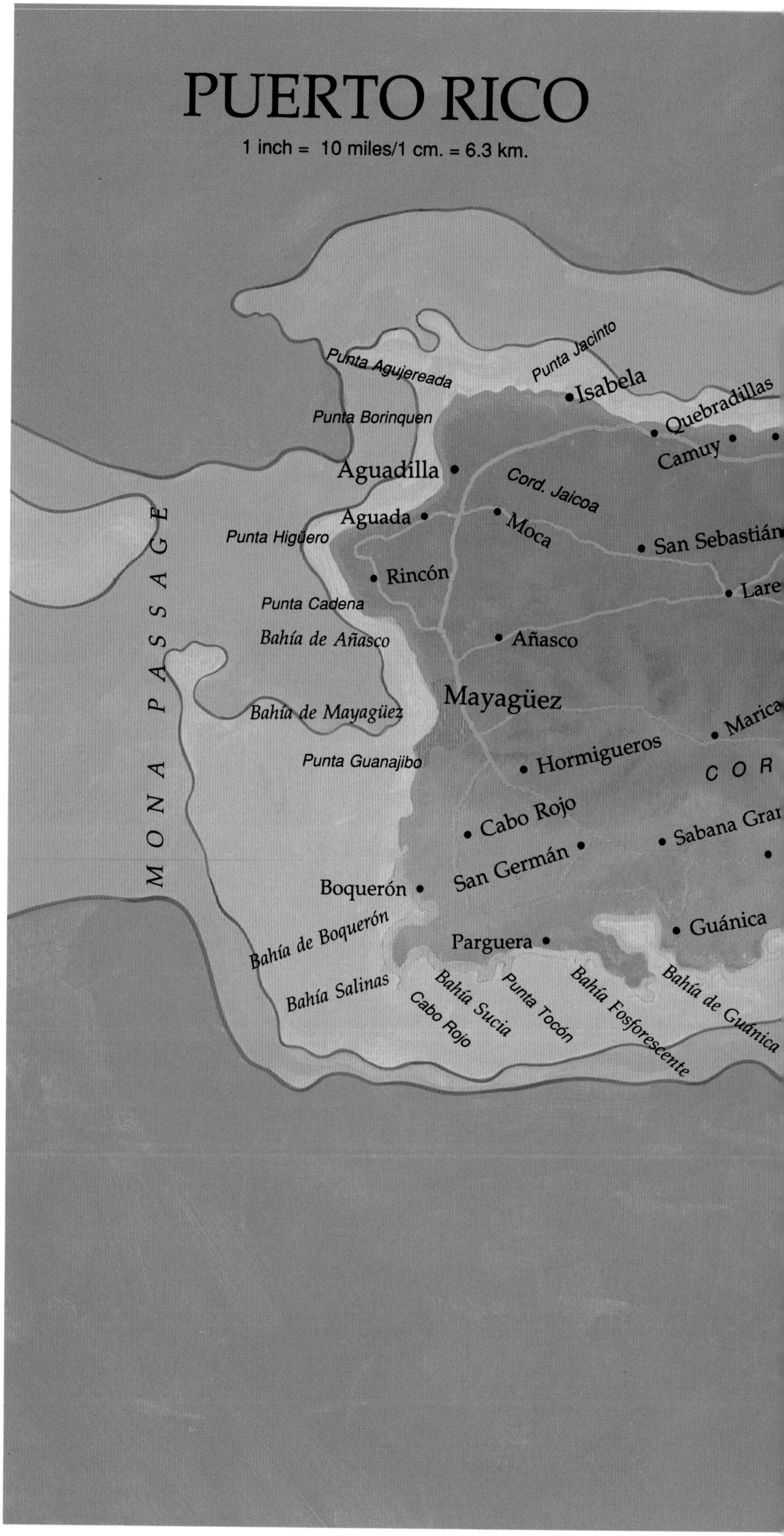

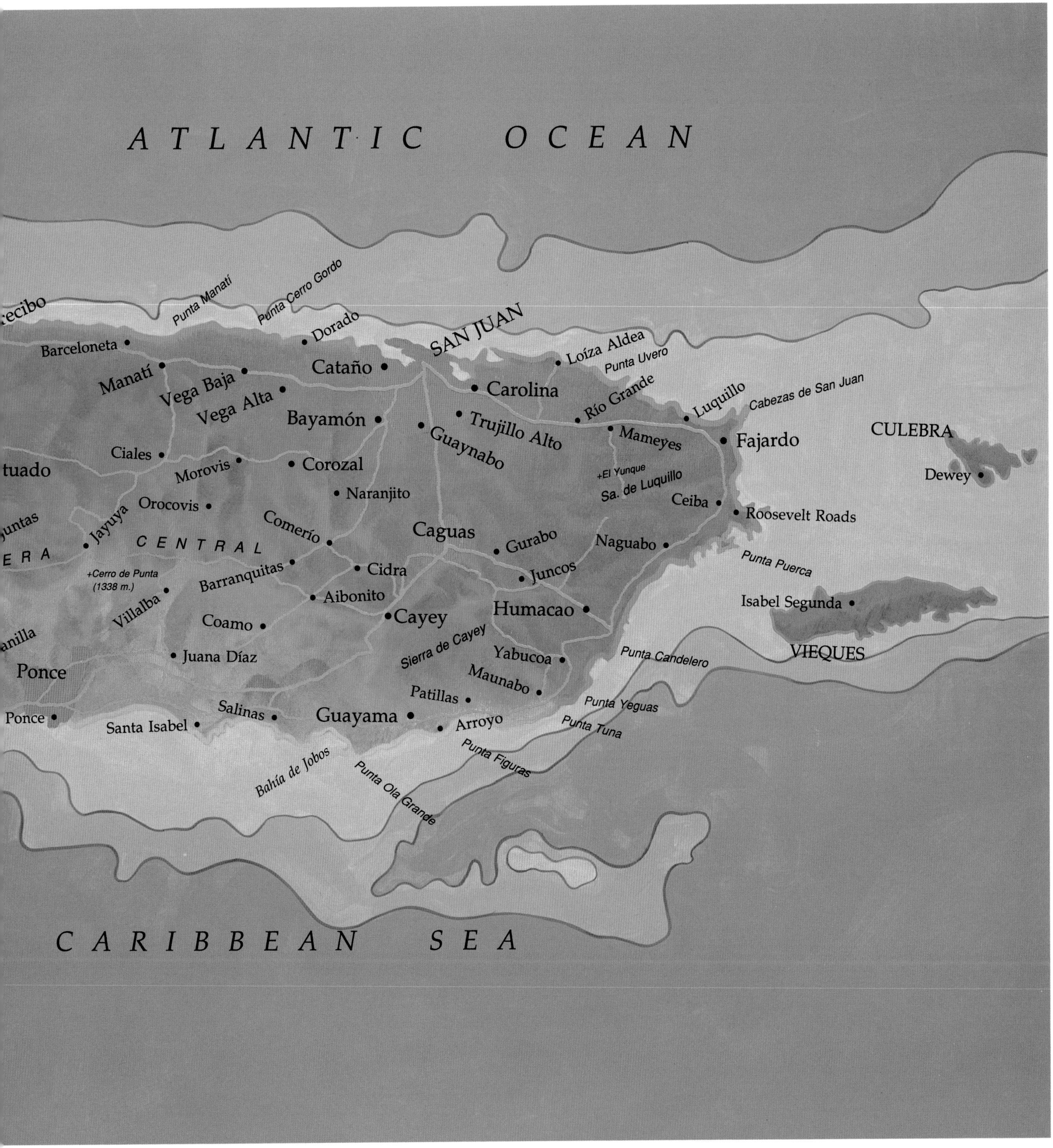

ATLANTIC OCEAN
recibo
Punta Manatí
Punta Cerro Gordo
Dorado
SAN JUAN
Barceloneta
Manatí
Vega Baja
Cataño
Vega Alta
Carolina
Loíza Aldea
Punta Uvero
Río Grande
Luquillo
Cabezas de San Juan
Bayamón
Trujillo Alto
Guaynabo
Mameyes
Fajardo
CULEBRA
Dewey
Ciales
tuado
Morovis
Corozal
+El Yunque
Sa. de Luquillo
Naranjito
Ceiba
Roosevelt Roads
Orocovis
Jayuya
juntas
ERA
CENTRAL
Comerío
Caguas
Gurabo
Naguabo
Punta Puerca
+Cerro de Punta
(1338 m.)
Barranquitas
Cidra
Juncos
Villalba
Aibonito
Humacao
Isabel Segunda
Coamo
Cayey
anilla
Sierra de Cayey
Yabucoa
Punta Candelero
VIEQUES
Juana Díaz
Ponce
Maunabo
Patillas
Punta Yeguas
Salinas
Guayama
Punta Tuna
Ponce
Santa Isabel
Arroyo
Punta Figuras
Bahía de Jobos
Punta Ola Grande
CARIBBEAN SEA

Acknowledgements

A book of this nature invariably owes a great deal to the generous cooperation of many people and organizations who have nothing to gain except the gratitude of the author, and perhaps, the intrinsic reward of assisting a book like this to publication. Walter Murray Chiesa again lent his invaluable advice and assistance while I was on location, and read over the text for accuracy. The contribution of many other individuals and organizations will be apparent from the text or from the credit lines at the photographs themselves, and I would like to express my gratitude to them, and also to:

Government of the Commonwealth of Puerto Rico; The Office of the Governor of Puerto Rico; Institute of Puerto Rican Culture; Conservation Trust of Puerto Rico; U.S. National Park Service; Library of Congress; Museum of the University of Puerto Rico; Río Camuy Caves; Museo de Arte de Ponce; Archivo General de Puerto Rico; Casa del Libro; Parque Zoológico de Mayagüez; Pueblo Supermarkets; Dorado Beach Hotel; Cerromar Beach Hotel; Caribe Hilton Hotel; Clarion Hotel; USDA Research Station, Mayagüez; Banco Popular; Abbott Laboratories; MDS Qantel; Galería Botello; U.S. Fish & Wildlife Service; Modern Graphics; Felix Garmendía; Luigi Marrozini; Myrna Baez; Terry Smrt; Ella LaBrucherie; and Martha Hoch. The map paintings were rendered by Patrick Waters of El Centro, California.

The photograph of the zemi on page 14 is courtesy of the National Museum of the American Indian/Smithsonian Institution.

Imágenes Press
Post Office Box 1150
Pine Valley, California 91962 USA
Tel: (619) 473-8676 / FAX: (619) 473-8272

Design consultant: HOCHdesigns, Los Angeles

Puerto Rico, Borinquen Querida
ISBN 0-939302-26-8 (Deluxe Edition)
ISBN 0-939302-27-6 (Presentation Edition)

Printed in China